The Many Deaths of Kristian 13

Yves Navant

The Many Deaths of Kristian 13

Yves Navant

Art direction and design: Yves Navant
Kristian 13 mural by
the amazing Victoriano Rivera

Photo by Yves Navant

This book is dedicated to anyone who falls in love with me after reading it. I survived all of this just to get to you.

-Yves Navant

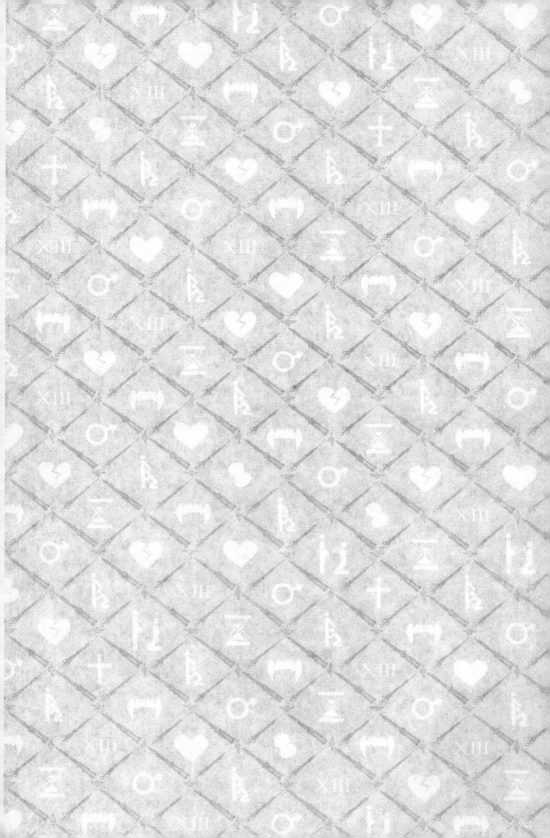

THE MANY DEATHS OF KRISTIAN 13

Prologue:

I can't believe you haven't heard this story.

I'm the youngest, the 13th of a remarkable family, a family of Gods and Monsters.

You'll see.

My father, Louis John the Baptiste Navant, was a villain; he was an angry, sometimes violent dictator that demanded total subservience from his family.

My father was a war hero, a member of the French Resistance and a renowned French chef. He helped liberate Southern France from German occupation, which is funny because he would eventually enslave my siblings and I under tyranny just as total and oppressive as any dished out by the Third Reich. My father was charming; he could put thoughts into your head, clouding your mind and force you to conform to his will. My father was just like Dracula, only French. I inherited my father's charisma, his ability to persuade and charm. I also inherited his angular, rather European good looks. I have an impossible face. Just like my dad. Louis' mind was a minefield; he could shift from roguish charm to apocalyptic rage in a heartbeat. As his son, I often found myself navigating that minefield.

My father was a villain, capable of grand and vicious acts of manipulation, cruelty and humiliation. In fact, if he hadn't been *my* father I'd have worshipped him. Just like Dracula.

My father met my mum, Ruth, and seduced her into marriage; he was 13 years older than her. My mum was a schoolteacher and the daughter of a German Minister. My mother was the antithesis of my father. Where Louis was a dark and charming manipulator, my beautiful mum was cherubic and genuine. The two of them offered an uneasy balance as parents; Ruth was the calm serenity at the heart of Louis' devastating storm.

My mum was expecting what she thought would be her last, 10th child when tragedy clawed at her. It was Christmas time and my family was busily preparing for the season and all its accompanying, requisite joy. One starless, frozen night in late December, my mum woke in agony and began to bleed uncontrollably. Ruth drove herself to the hospital; doctors administered drugs intended to halt a dangerously early birth. The drugs failed and Ruth was faced with an impossible decision, save her life at the cost of her unborn child's. Turns out fate made Ruth's choice for her; labor started and neither medicine or pleading prayer could stop it. Late one winter night, all alone in a hospital, my mum lost the baby. Ruth wanted that child to be her last; doctors told her it *should* have been her last.

I said Ruth drove herself to the hospital; she was alone. Of course a skeletal crew of doctors and nurses were present at that hour of the night, but my dad didn't come. He never went to the hospital for any of his children's births. This awful night was no different. My heartbroken mum sat in her room and tried to catch her breath. When I was older, mum would tell me of her sweeping sadness as she listened to the cries of other babies who survived to be born just a few yards away, babies that were being comforted by their new mothers in neighboring rooms. It was Christmastime, my mum was served a meal, there was a small, felt elf decoration on the tray; a tiny, happy symbol of yuletide optimism standing in contrast to the crushing disaster that had just occurred. Every year my mum hung that elf on her Christmas tree; at first I thought he looked cheap and garish next to the opulence her taste usually demanded. I once commented on my distaste for the shabby elf, my mum told me the story of the elf's origin. Every Christmas I look for that elf and take a second to silently wish the sibling I don't have a happy holiday.

Almost a year after losing the baby, against doctor's orders and in defiance of fate, my mum and dad took the chance to conceive another child. My mother had no intention of allowing destiny to take from her what she had planned. Her pregnancy was difficult but my mum continued with her everyday life unimpeded and willful. After nine long months, at the height of summer Ruth visited her doctor's office for a regular check up. Ruth was seated in the waiting room when she calmly told the receptionist she had gone into labor. Luckily the office was conjoined with the hospital and they quickly wheeled Ruth to a delivery room. The doctor turned his back on my mum to wash his hands and put gloves on, but there was no time. With a first exhibition of its characteristic urgency and impatience, the baby was on its way. In the early afternoon, on a sunny, warm day at the end of June, Ruth Navant gave birth to her final child, Louis' 13th. This was the environment I arrived into.

With a quiet sigh, I was born.

A COUPLE OF LION CUBS
Photo by Victoria Coco

Chapter 1: THE BOY WHO FELL TO EARTH

When I was little I had pet lions and tigers.

As a chef my dad made the acquaintance of taxidermists and furriers, members of the Safari Club International. Through those friends my father acquired several rare and endangered animals that he would bring home to us as pets: lions, one full grown and one cub, a tiger cub, antelope kept in a pen in the backyard and once, even a shark in our bathtub. Sometimes the animals didn't stay long, but I was the only little kid at my school with a pet tiger.

My dad was larger than life. Louis could've been the coolest father; I could have grown up idolizing him, but the memories of him at his worst cut into me and left indelible scars. When I was small, I loved my dad. Even at so young an age as 3 or 4, I knew everyone else was afraid of him. I hadn't yet been on the receiving end of my father's aggression. All in good time.

My father raised us to expect an enemy invasion or a terrorist attack. Having survived the Nazi occupation of France, my traumatized father stood in wait for any possible recurrence. My father rarely slept, I rarely ever remember a genuine smile on his face. If he ever smiled it was in cruel satisfaction. My father wanted us to be prepared to face what he had seen; he wanted the mettle of our spirits to be forged in the flames he'd survived. I was lectured on guerilla tactics and military strategy. I can't ride a bike or throw a ball; I didn't learn those kinds of things. That's not who my father was, that's not the kind of childhood I had.

I grew up in Colorado, in a small suburb west of Denver. My

hometown, Golden, was a mash up of old west clichés and modern development. I always drew, that was my favorite pastime; I drew. If I wasn't drawing, I was reading. My dad would stand behind me and watch what I was doing, after assessing my art he'd roughly rub the top of my head.

If the devil had a son named Kristian, he *would* love him.

I speak from experience.

My mum soon got a job outside our home, she wanted a bit of freedom. I was left in the care of an older sister, Monique. One day Monique left me alone in our very big, very dark, seemingly ancient Victorian style home. Monique said she was going to get the mail, she told me to keep the lights off so kidnappers wouldn't know I was inside. It was the first time I had been left alone; I felt anxiety rise in my little, four-year-old chest. Every sound was terrifying, every noise was one of the aforementioned kidnappers, and every creak was a monster coming to devour me. I had to get out of the house; I thought I had a better chance out in the open than trapped inside.

I managed to open the heavy front door and peered outside, making sure a hulking, disfigured killer wasn't waiting for me on the front step. The bright sun overwhelmed my eyes. I glanced around the yard and found the coast to be clear. I looked up and down the street for any sign of Monique, she was nowhere in sight. I panicked and began to run down the street, headed in the general direction of my mum's work.

I looked back to see how far I'd run, I couldn't see my house. I began to cry. I tried to run faster; my chest burned, I just wanted to get to my mum. An approaching car slowed as I ran, the driver's window came down and I knew this was it; this was going to be the moment where I was kidnapped. I'd never see my family again. I'd been caught by a child-snatcher.

From inside the car a warm voice said, "Are you Kristian Navant?"

It was the Avon lady; my salvation came at the hands of my neighborhood Avon lady. The woman with her vivid, Technicolor face paint recognized me and took me home. The brightly painted Avon lady sat with me on my front step till Monique returned from her mysterious and lengthy trip to "get the mail".

That was my very first experience with uncontrollable horror. It made my stomach hurt and it made me cry. I felt unreasoning panic and I tried desperately to regain control but couldn't.

I loved the feeling. I did *not* love that I had been abandoned.

I see now why the teenage babysitters get killed in horror films. Negligent bitches.

LIFE IN THE HOUSE OF N.
Photo by Victoria Coco

Chapter 2: PLEASANT VIEW ELEMENTARY CONFIDENTIAL

I started school at Pleasant View Elementary shortly after my fourth birthday. I had an advantage over the other kids my age, my sister Michiko taught me to read and write before entering kindergarten. I cut my literary teeth on the hallucinogenic world of Doctor Seuss and quickly moved on to comic books. I was fascinated by the melodrama and violence of comics, and also by the skintight costumes worn by impossibly beautiful men and strong women. I experienced my first kiss in kindergarten. A girl named Lydia and I decided we were married; we spent an afternoon making out inside the oversize tires on the playground.

I loved to learn and I loved to assert myself. My mind was a voracious animal, devouring everything it could. School soon became an issue; I had no patience. I'd finish my work, leave my assigned desk and attempt to help classmates with theirs. My kindergarten teacher kept me in from recess because of my penmanship; my mum taught me to finish lower-case A's with a curly tail, my teacher hated it. I refused to submit to her will, I refused to turn my back on what my mother had taught me. I'd rather miss recess.

My siblings and I were always encouraged by our mother to dream, to use our imaginations. Everyday before school I was a vampire, rising from my shadowy crypt and every afternoon I was a superhero, fighting crime before dinner. On weekends, I was a spaceman saving an alien world from scientific disaster. My brother Jacques and I would make costumes out of butcher paper. We made ray guns and smoke bombs. Together Jacques and I walked through post-apocalyptic, irradiated wastelands and alien jungles. Our imaginations were wonderful, terrible things, honed to absolute perfection.

I lived for Halloween and the ensuing costume party at school; my mum was an amazing seamstress. My alter ego was most often a vampire; I kept plastic fangs with me year round. Dracula was a role model; dark, charming, charismatic, willful and ambitious, like my dad but without the hitting. Thanks Bela Lugosi.

It was in First Grade that I was offered my first professional art job. I was paid to illustrate a children's cookbook, I drew the requested illustrations in a tongue-in-cheek manner, stylizing and cartooning wherever possible. I knew my ability to draw made me special, it made me more than the other kids and I reveled in it. My work was popular enough that a teacher from a neighboring school asked me to draw similar material for her. I was paid $5 for the second job, which I quickly spent on Masters of the Universe toys.

I love the memory of that event, Kristian Navant, a paid illustrator at 6 years old. If I had known the realities of a sustained career in art, I'd have pursued politics. Or cult leadership.

Starting when I was 8 years old I'd send Mattel and Hasbro, the makers of Masters of the Universe and G.I. Joe respectively, designs for new toys I'd created. I had found the address for each company on the packages of action figures, I drew designs for characters I thought would make good toys and sent them off in the mail with a brief, childishly hopeful letter of introduction. I was so optimistic and creative; even then I was consumed by the intensity and aspiration within me. Weeks later I would receive letters on the company stationary, thanking me for the design and praising my ambition. I was overjoyed to be recognized for the effort. I once phoned the offices of Marvel Comics to tell them all about a heroine I'd created that I thought perfect for their books. I was 9.

Pleasant View Elementary had an epic library, complete with a full size Viking ship. Kids could climb inside and read in silence. My happiest moments at Pleasant View were spent in that Viking ship, in solitude, away from the other children. Or in the art room, I loved the art room and it's rotating cast of teachers: hippies, weirdoes and bohemians.

Third grade was my last good year at school. My teacher, Mrs. Jones, was a wild mix of gypsy and self-help guru; she nurtured my creative side to a fault, allowing me to disregard my other academic duties. One January afternoon I was sitting at my desk when Mrs. Jones entered the room in tears; she was hysterical. I felt uneasy. Mrs. Jones stood at the front of the room and tried to speak, choking back tears. I began to assume the worst. Kids in my class tried to comfort our teacher as she attempted to rally, restraining her emotions. Finally, after a brutal few moments, Mrs. Jones said, "There's been a terrible disaster…"

Before she could finish speaking, a flood of tears once more overcame Mrs. Jones. I immediately deduced what could cause such a breakdown: nuclear war. We'd been bombed by the Soviets. Or someone. One of America's enemies had finally struck at us on our own soil and now we all had to pay the price, just like my dad had foreseen, just like my father taught us to expect. I tried to remember what dad taught me, I tried to recall how to handle myself in a hostile invasion. I couldn't remember what he said about nuclear bombardment. Fuck. I couldn't remember.

I just *knew* that's what had happened, Mrs. Jones had heard the awful news and came in to report it to my class. Mrs. Jones sobbed at the front of the classroom. I thought of my mum, I quickly decided I'd wrap myself in plastic bags from the class room's garbage to shield myself from the fallout. I'd try to walk home through the inevitable dead and dying littering the streets. I knew I had to cover my skin, eyes, nose and mouth. I thought about Christmases and how I'd miss them. I hoped that my mum was still alive; I prayed she'd be okay. I prayed I'd make it home. I knew I'd miss cartoons and comic books and life as it had been up till that afternoon. I braced myself for the moment when I'd be cast out into the debris and poisonous, irradiated destruction outside.

Mrs. Jones choked, "The space shuttle Challenger just exploded, the astronauts were all killed…"

Some of the boys and girls in my class started to cry. Nasa's Challenger had exploded 73 seconds into its flight over the Atlantic Ocean, just off the coast of Florida. Mrs. Jones had been watching the launch with other teachers and returned to our classroom in hysterics. The Challenger had exploded.

"Thank God!" I thought, "It was just the space shuttle."

The rest of my time in the public school system was a nightmare.

I had few, if any supportive teachers and as puberty began to rear it's dangerous head I grew further apart from my peers. I had no friends, a mutual decision made by my classmates and myself. As my body began its chrysalis from child to adolescent, my mind began to change as well. I knew I wasn't interested in sports or whatever other tedious activities kids in my class enjoyed. I wanted to read and draw and daydream. I wanted to be the star in a story of my own conception. I wanted to be a deadly super villain. I wanted to be Emperor of the world. The other boys wanted to play catch.

I began to hear phrases like "Faggot" and "Queer" with increasing frequency. I was hunted before and after school. Lunch and recess became a Darwinist nightmare. I lived for the privacy of my bedroom, where I could flee into fiction and art once the school day ended.

The remainder of my time in elementary school was a prison sentence. I was passing through the educational system like something indigestible through a human body, like a piece of glass accidently eaten.

Chapter 3: WARTIME LIFE ON THE HOME FRONT

Monsters from space make good families. Sometimes.

I had never been the target of my father's fury, but I'd seen it. I lived my life in fear of his rage; I walked on glass, waiting for a crack to emerge under my weight. As a child I was filled with constant anxiety that my father would explode, he threatened to bludgeon my mother with a heavy gold candlestick, he'd force us to sit in silence without lights or television, he refused to allow us to celebrate holidays, especially Christmas, till he was out of the house. I could relate innumerable vile and wicked things my father did, abuse he subjected my family to, but I won't. This isn't his story; it's mine.

The first time my father struck me was with a rolled up newspaper, the evening edition became a baton. I don't even remember what I did, probably something every little kid does. However, the afternoon I began to hate my father was on a day without a grand and operatic display of his signature fury. My father calmly followed me through the house after I had caused a disruption; I sat down in the living room amid a number of my siblings, my mother was there. I thought I was safe among so many witnesses. My father calmly approached me; his mouth was a perfectly straight line and his eyes were cold, black pools. In one fluid gesture my father slapped my face with enough force to topple me to my side, like a lion pawing at its prey. I immediately forced myself upright. I screamed silently to myself. I didn't want to show any external sign of emotion. My cheek throbbed; my eyes burned and betrayed me. Stinging tears leapt from my eyes like cliff divers. I was embarrassed. Humiliated. My face ached, but the pain of being victimized in front of my brothers and sisters was worse. I didn't mind if my father beat me, he could have killed me, as long as none of my siblings watched.

I was hounded, harassed and bullied everyday at school. Now I'd been humiliated in my own home.

It was in that exact moment I began to loathe my father. Though I'm sure the embers had been there all along, a flame had ignited inside of me and no matter what I did, I couldn't put it out.

There were very rare occasions when my father would exhibit odd, out of character tenderness, once comforting me after a bad dream. I was certain no monster or boogey man could be as terrifying as my father, I was safe so long as I could hear my father pacing the floors while I lay in bed.

My dad was a liar.

I was reading a comic on our front step one spring evening, the setting sun lit the world on fire and the sky above me was the color of gold and rust. It was warm outside and I could hear my mum inside the house raising her voice to my father. Someone suddenly becoming brave enough to stand up to my father was a rare occasion, so I knew something extreme was going on. My courageous mother angrily confronted my father; he sat emotionless, staring past her, looking right through her. My stomach began to hurt, as if I were on a too-fast amusement park ride or standing atop a very tall building. I dreaded what would come next, would my father break things? Would he hurt my mother? Would he hurt *me*?

I crept close to an open window and listened. My mum had discovered a very carefully hidden secret of my father's; he had been married before, he had three daughters prior to meeting Ruth. My eldest sister was born of a wartime romance; the following pair came from a woman Louis married as a young man and mysteriously lost interest in around the same time as meeting Ruth. Louis had the audacity to name the first girl he and Ruth had after a previous daughter, Michele. Louis missed his original daughters, but not enough to tell my mother those girls existed, and not enough to act like their father. Thus my position as Louis' 13th, and last child.

If a parent never exhibits vulnerability, their children stop thinking of them as human. Wait. I can't say I ever stopped thinking of my dad as human, because I never started.

When I was 10, my father had surgery to remove an aneurism.

A few nights after the surgery my mum escorted me to see my father as he recovered in the hospital. He'd be coming home on Thanksgiving Day. We entered the same hospital where I was born and approached the wing my father was being kept in. It was evening and traffic in the hospital was light, the walls were starkly white. Everything was starkly white.

The door to my father's room was open just a crack. A nurse stepped out of the room, looking down as she passed us. I turned my head to watch as she walked purposefully down the corridor. Faint yellow light crept out of my father's room, it looked like it was trying to escape, but the light had been fatally wounded and was now reduced to a crawl.

My mother took the lead and slowly stepped inside the room, it was supposed to be white. I *know* hospitals are all white and silver, but it looked as though this room had been cloaked in oppressive shadows. At the epicenter of the gloom lay my father. He was grey and faded but he was still my father; the same man I described earlier, only now he was a photograph left in the sun. He seemed drained; he had a mere fraction of his terrible intensity. My father was at the center of a mechanical spider's web, attached to countless machines and monitors. Wires and tubes were attached to his very veins, running from his nose, from his ears and chest; chords ran everywhere. Like a special effect in a futuristic film, the surrounding automations spoke in a series of drips, beeps and electronic stutters. It was hard to discern where my father ended and the machines began. His breath sounded dry, labored and ragged, like part of his will was focused and concentrated on breathing. Each breath sounded like dry leaves rustling inside a metal casket.

I stumbled toward my father's bed as he greeted my mother; he noticed my presence as I approached. Mum gave me a polite verbal introduction and he turned his eye toward me. I stepped closer, astounded by the impossibility of all of this. My fierce and ferocious father laid low and now reliant on machinery. I noticed small, dried tracks of blood running from his ears. My grey, mechanical father did something that shocked me; he reached out his huge, cold, frail hand and rubbed the top of my head, as roughly as his trembling form was able. For the first time since I was a very small child, he mussed my hair and smiled at me. I looked at his wrist and the tubes connected to him under a concealing bandage and followed their path up his arm to his body, to his face. I was horrified and uncomfortable. My father was smiling; his was a satisfied, content smile.

Father spoke my name in his heavy, distinctive accent, made even more remarkable by the effect his condition had on his voice; it sounded like a recording of his normal self being played back on a damaged device. I don't remember what he said to me, only the sound.

My father was brought home on Thanksgiving. I watched out a window as he approached the house. I thought to myself, "Nothing will kill him."

Chapter 4: RED HOT THROBBING NEON AND THE PERPETUAL FEVER

Puberty.

Sexual maturity came at me like a dog in heat.

Maybe I was an early developer, but Batgirl made me hump myself to a dry, little prepubescent orgasm more times than I can count. Or Robin. And Robin.

Once the atomic furnace of puberty began to seethe inside of me, it was all I could do to control it. I began to think about sex all the time; any kind of sex, all kinds of sex. Sex seemed like a perfectly dangerous amusement park and I wanted to ride every ride. My 5th and 6th grade teachers used health films to instill an oppressive paranoia of STDs, specifically AIDS.

I had a perpetual erection, but the shadow of fear was constantly looming over me. I'd get so worked up, running mini-films in my mind of all the dirty, amazing, awful, wonderful things I wanted to do and skin I needed to touch that I'd need to relieve the tension. Masturbation was an art form and like a true artist, I practiced it anywhere I could; school, the park, the mall. After finally experiencing the sweet, blessed relief of ejaculation, I'd be racked by a guilty conscious until the next inevitable erection.

I was in 6th grade when my slick, red chrysalis of puberty began. My class and I were returning from gym class and some of the boys and I were roughhousing in the hall. One blonde boy named Jeff and I roughhoused a little longer than the others; he was a soccer player, his family knew my family. We were all being herded through the halls, being led back to our classroom and I needed to stop by the little boy's room to pee. Jeff and I continued to mock fight and jump on each other. This ill-advised body contact continued, Jeff followed me into the bathroom. I told him to get lost, as I really did have to go. He refused and tried to force his way into my stall, we were both laughing hysterically.

Jeff was trying to wedge his body into my stall as I tried to close the door, he gave up and I thought he had left. I opened my jeans, lowering my briefs and suddenly the door flung open behind me. I yanked my briefs back up, but something made it impossible to put them back in place; I'm pretty sure it was all the roughhousing that made my young cock hard.

I turned to push the door shut and saw Jeff, who had been laughing up till that second. Jeff was staring at my cock, he wasn't laughing anymore. Jeff looked up and we made eye contact for a brief second before he lowered his eyes once more. I tried to put my now painfully erect dick back in place, but I couldn't make it behave; it jutted awkwardly from the leg of my briefs.

"I can still see it…" Jeff said, he sounded kind of dazed.

We both just stood there, Jeff staring at my dick and me staring at Jeff's awestruck face. After a few eternal moments, Jeff stumbled backward and left the bathroom. I turned back to the toilet and lowered my briefs. I remember thinking, "That was cool."

Throughout the next few years, my raging hormones set the pace for the rest of my life. I've heard stories about the flickering, greasy neon of puberty coming on like a quick fever and then settling down once the body matures. This was not the case with me. Once sex took hold of my mind, it never let go. I had contracted the guilty, gratifying sickness of sex and found no cure.

Though admittedly, the fever was the worst in Jr. High. I wanted any contact I could get. I pursued it. I chased after it like a ravenous animal. There was a girl named Nikki, she had legs longer and whiter and more perfect than something that had starved itself on a fashion catwalk. In fact, that was her nickname: Legs. I suppose everyone loved her. She and I were walking down the hall one day and I was playing the role of the brooding, misunderstood youth.

I made some remark about how a girl like her could never like me; her Disney-Princess-esque concern took over as I assumed it would. Nikki immediately began to console me. I think I actually asked for a kiss on the cheek, just to prove I was as human as she. As Nikki moved in for an innocent peck, I turned my face to kiss her back. My first real kiss; stolen in the empty halls of my Jr. High, while everyone else was in class. I couldn't wait to replay the kiss in my mind, slowing the film down so I could prolong it.

On another day, I excused myself from Mr. Cochran's math class just to get away, just to roam the halls. While haunting the corridors like a sex-starved ghost, I realized my penis was erect and thought that specific moment was a splendid time to masturbate. I had my choice of locations in which to stroke off; the locker room was out because it was damp and hot. Too hot. The bathrooms further inside the belly of the school were ok, but they all had typical stalls, no real excitement there. Completely enclosed, private stalls. Yawn. My very favorite location was the boy's room just above the gym, a brick and porcelain miracle of modern plumbing. The stalls of that bathroom were simple brick partitions between each toilet. No doors. I wasn't sure why my already hard cock twitched at the layout of that room, but it did.

I stepped inside and walked to the stall farthest against the back wall. Once you were inside, there was no coverage from others in the room. Whatever you were doing was on clear display, in plain view of anyone in the bathroom. You could also see inside the stalls from the mirrors above the sinks. I stood in front of the toilet and began to jack off; soon I heard rustling outside. I stopped my rapid manipulations and tried to control my breathing. I looked around but saw no one. I turned my body; I now faced outward, away from the toilet. I continued, moving my hand up and down the length of my shaft. I smiled to myself, deducing what the rustling had meant. Fear and nervousness drove up my spine like a racecar, dirty immodesty and hesitant exhibitionism rode shotgun. After a few seconds, the mysterious rustling resumed. I began to pose while I stroked, as if being photographed; I moved intentionally, like I was being watched. I heard more rustling and very, very hushed whispers. A devilish smirk crossed my mouth and I sped my movements toward crescendo.

The whispers continued, as did the rustling. Breathing that sounded heaver than it should have been echoed in a rasp, and the breathing wasn't coming from me. I blasted across the bathroom like a pistol, the absence of a stall door allowed my genetic filth to hit the sink facing me. I regained my composure and tried to halt the convulsions that shook my chest.

I stepped out of the bathroom to find two classmates, Jeff Something and Matt Something-that-started-with-an-R, standing outside staring like spectators at a circus. They both had bright red cheeks and these awful, idiotic smiles on their faces. They both kind of giggled and as I walked past, I made sure to make eye contact and smile at them.

"Did… did you have fun in there?" Matt Whatever-his-name-was asked, his voice sounded like he might be thirsty, he sounded just a little breathless. Matt stuttered like a trauma victim as he tried to speak. Both lads looked at me like witnesses to a car crash or a miracle. Or both. I fucking loved it.

As I moved beside and past them, I cocked my head back in acknowledgement of their presence. I walked back to class feeling awful and guilty and excited. I felt accomplished and satisfied. I sat back down and finished my day.

As I was sitting there, surrounded by mindless drones and a tedious teacher, one thought kept replaying in my head: "That was so cool."

Chapter 5: SAVE US FROM THESE FACELESS KNIGHTS OF SUBURBIA

I hated Junior High.

I attended school in a brick and mortar prison, Bell Junior High: where individuality went to die. My alienation and isolation developed in tandem with my body; it was in junior high that I realized the seemingly awful truth about myself, that I was a sexual deviant. I never tried to hide my nebulous, undefined sexual preferences. That made me the target of my peers.

I was harassed in the halls, called faggot, queer, whatever. Classmates broke into my locker and stole my gym clothes, putting them in the toilet. My legs were pulled out from under me as I walked up a crowded staircase. I was hunted every minute of the day.

Everyday was a nightmare. Every, single day.

I *did* try to seek help and sanctuary from school counselors. "Officials". I begged school officials to help me, to do something, to do *anything*. Their answer was to sit around all day and think of new ways to do nothing while I was being devoured.

I thought I was the only boy feeling what I was feeling. I thought I was alone. On the worst days, on the days that the harassment began the second I stepped on school grounds and threatened to overwhelm me, I'd run away. I'd leave the spirit-crushing environment of my junior high and spend the day roaming around my town. I'd wander the streets and shops like a ghost, a directionless phantom.

I'd return to the school parking lot in time for the final bell, in time to get picked up by my mum, never having been to class. I'd get home and sink into the safety of my bedroom. I cursed myself for not being brave enough to kill myself.

Anyone who believes sexual deviancy is an elective, chosen path should be killed. I should kill you myself.

I knew I was something rare and exceptional. Since I was an alien, a monster, a one of a kind creature, I had to protect myself. I was an endangered species, possibly the last of my breed. My injured spirit had begun to glow, the dying embers that had been all but snuffed out by the abuse of my bastard, mongrel peers and useless school "resources" had been fanned into a tiny inferno. My peers had unknowingly baptized me in fire. My soul was molten metal and my life was the anvil I was forged against. With every insult, with every push, shove and slur, my peers and the world around them made me razor sharp and strong. They made me unbeatable. Indestructible.

I had suffered to become what I was, and I was *so **much** more* than those around me.

Chapter 6: And Hungry Graves Shall Finally Claim Their Dead

While I was busy surviving junior high, my father's rage grew exponentially.

My father refused to let us decorate for Christmas; my mum defied him. Louis accused Ruth of sleeping around, of seeing other men; he was paranoid and delusional. To the credit of Ruth's character and the detriment of her common sense, she never became involved with another man. Ruth mated for life. Like a swan.

One Sunday was worse than others; Louis confronted Ruth with insane accusations of infidelity. My father shouted at my mother, he spit at her, he grabbed her and threw her to the floor. My father yanked our phone from the wall and smashed it. I saw my father do all of this and could do nothing to stop it.

I prayed for my father's death. I begged God to reach down with wrath and vengeance and cleanse the blight of my father from our lives. I begged.

Jacques woke me up early one Saturday morning, it had snowed lightly the night before but it was now bright and sunny. So much so that the morning sun burst into my room like an unwanted intruder and burned my eyes as they struggled to adjust to waking life. It was the morning of April 13th. I was 13 years old.

"Wanna see something weird?" Jacques spoke like he wasn't certain whether or not he was joking.

I agreed and Jacques led me to our bathroom, he very carefully and quietly opened the door just enough to reveal our father. Our father was lying on his back on the floor in front of the sink; he *seemed* to be sleeping. I was certain that if Jacques and I made a sound, our father would leap up and attack us for waking him. I was sure that my father's whole performance was a subterfuge devised to test us; if Jacques and I had the gall to disturb dad's feigned slumber, he'd have an excuse to punish us.

Jacques and I quietly closed the door and went in to the living room to wait. "I hope he stops soon, cause I really wanna take a shower." I remarked to Jacques.

Jacques and I waited a seeming eternity; finally we lost patience and called our sister Thea for help. Thea lived across town, but said she was on her way; she arrived and called paramedics. The paramedics called my mum, who rushed home from a class at a nearby college campus.

I was ushered upstairs, away from the paramedics and emergency responders. I knew what was going on downstairs; these well-intended strangers were working feverishly to revive my father. Our father was unresponsive. I crossed my fingers and silently prayed. I prayed for God to hear me and grant my wish, I prayed for my father to finally die.

I became impatient and had to see what was going on. If something was actually able to strike my father down, I wanted to see it for myself. I wanted to see my father with my own eyes. I wanted to experience my father's defeat. I had to.

I purposefully walked downstairs. I stopped in the doorway between the kitchen and our living room, paramedics were packing up their gear and members of my family were positioned throughout the room. Mum was sitting at the dinner table, Thea stood across from her, rubbing her closed eyes. Surely Thea wasn't fighting back tears. No one would cry for our father. I certainly wouldn't. I don't remember for certain where anyone else was, just mum and Thea. Mum had her back to me.

Finally I saw what I had been waiting for; the sight I had pleaded and prayed and bargained for. I looked down at my father, lying still in the center of the room. I looked at my father just in time to see paramedics pulling a light blue sheet over his body.

The sheet was lovely and fit the room perfectly. It was a matte, pale blue that matched the décor wonderfully. Mum had recently redecorated and the living room was now all whites and light blues. I don't know if anyone else noticed, but I certainly applauded my mother's intuitive foresight. This was one of our family's most cinematically surreal and pivotal moments and the stage was set perfectly. Just perfectly.

"Where is Kristian?" Mum's concerned voice broke my reverie.

"I'm right here." I announced.

Mum turned to see me standing in the doorway, she instructed me to head back upstairs. Assuming I would react traditionally to the scene unfolding, Mum didn't want me to see my father being carried out to the coroner's meat wagon. I initially refused to comply but finally obeyed and returned to the second floor. I had seen enough. I had the visual confirmation I wanted.

That afternoon my family gathered in a solemn mood. I spoke out in optimism and excitement for the future, for which I was verbally chastised. Evidently it was too early to celebrate my father's death. Oh well, I thought. I could wait. I'd waited this long. The first night was difficult, not because the obvious absence of my father. Everyone had gone out except mum and myself. We were alone with a very fresh ghost. That night was difficult because I saw my father everywhere, in every shadow. I saw my father in every corner; he was outside in the darkness, he was sitting on his bed as I passed by.

My father's body was to be flown to California and buried in a cemetery outside of Los Angeles. The cemetery was where his mother, a classically scary French crone was buried. Mum and Thea were to escort my father's body to the coast. I asked to go with them, my request was denied. I just wanted to see California.

Before dad's final plane ride, a viewing was planned for his body in Colorado. Most of my siblings went to pay their last respects to our father; everyone except Jacques, he refused to go. I remember some of the older siblings asking if I needed a moment before I entered the warmly lit room in the mortuary where my father was laid. I didn't. I just wanted to see him one more time, to make sure he was dead; really, truly, finally dead. I walked in and there my father was, in a majestic blue metal casket; he wore a dark suit and I could tell he was wearing a bit of makeup. Tall lamps stood on either side of his casket and white drapery hung all around, like some roman alter, lost in time. Flowers and greenery were placed nearby in tasteful displays. Even then, in that gross moment of finality, I was certain he'd spring up and begin shouting. I was ready for him to return to life and destroy us all.

The one thing I couldn't understand was the behavior of my brothers and sisters. Some of my older siblings wrote messages to our father and put them in his coffin. They wrote heartfelt letters about how they'd miss him, about how sorry they were. Things *normal* kids would do for *normal* parents. Fools. That wasn't us. Didn't they see how free we could all be now? Didn't they realize that our lives could finally begin?

Can you just imagine? Those rash emotional missteps, those misguided heart-to-hearts will be entombed with our father forever. They'll never get those words back. They'll never get to exhume our father and write a what-I-meant-to-say-was addendum.

I wasn't going to poor my heart out to a dead man. Especially not one I was sure could return at any time to resume his reign of tyranny and terror.

I've never cried over my father's death. Ever. Not a single tear.

Chapter 7: I WAS A TEENAGE SPACE VAMPIRE

High school was a necessary evil.

The only redeeming aspects of high school were my Advanced Placement art classes, and the school's mascot, the Demon. Other than those very small caveats, Golden Senior High embodied all the same idiotic trappings as every other American high school. It was the altar, upon which youthful dreams and ambitions were sacrificed, replaced by a hunger for anonymity and conformity. I had grown quite comfortable in my skin and enjoyed standing out; I was the exception to the rule of the self-conscious teen. I never wanted to be the boy next door.

Hungry for nightlife and adventure, I added years to the birth date on my student I.D. to get into dance clubs. Guests had to be 16 to qualify as all-ages; I was merely 14. There were two legendary clubs, Rock Island in the heart of pre-gentrified Denver and Ground Zero in college town Boulder. Both were havens for punks, Goths, rivet heads, rude boys, mods and skinheads. Random strays would pass through as well, the preppy kids sneaking away from their keggers and date rapes for a walk on the wild side. But, those two clubs belonged to the city's youthful scary monsters. The loud music and hedonism drew me like a post-pubescent moth toward flames of passion and possible violence.

I had met a tall, explosive native-American boy named Jeremy at school. Jeremy was an impossible mix of feminine characteristics and a hardened exterior; he was the toughest queer I'd ever meet. We became friends immediately. Freshman year wound down and school was out for summer.

My wonderfully indulgent mum flew Jacques and I to California to visit our eldest brother Jean Pierre and to visit our father's grave. I dreaded flying; very few activities fill me with such an overpowering terror. I miraculously survived the flight and stepped off the plane and into the moist night air of the west coast. I loved California. No other place seemed to mirror the duality I felt inside: cinematic hope and promise, sleeping right next to debased, thrill seeking cheapness.

The high and also low point of our holiday was a trip to Disneyland. Jean and his wife insisted we go to the legendary theme park. I rode a single ride but I *loved* Disneyland.

I think I was 15 when we went on that trip. Yes, I had just turned 15.

My family strolled Disneyland's main drag; the sensory overload was tangible, I could reach out and touch a cartoon come to life. It was around dinnertime. Mum and Jean Pierre chose a suitable place to eat, a Disneyland restaurant in French Café drag. The hostess seated us on an outdoor patio. I felt heat rise from somewhere low and dangerous as our waiter approached. He was handsome, in his late teens or early twenties and wore black-rimmed glasses. Like Buddy Holly. I can't remember what color his eyes were, but I remember liking them. His lips were pink and perfect and curled up in just the right spots, at the far corner on each side. I was 15.

My eyes were tiny cameras and the waiter soon realized he was being photographed. We made eye contact from across the distance and I realized the waiter and I were speaking the same language. When he brought our food the waiter let his body graze against my hand as it rested on the edge of the table. The heat inside of me spiked so quickly it threatened to overwhelm my senses. I could *smell* the waiter, clean and young, but so warm.

I could smell him.

My family finished their meal and returned to the park, I waited till they were in yet another lengthy, monotonous line and broke free. The second I knew I was out of sight from my family's point of view, I ran back to the café. I posed outside the café, waiting for the waiter to walk outside and see me. I waited a breathless forever, till the waiter finally appeared, serving tables. My breath felt hot, like I had a fever. I psychically whispered to him, "Look at me."

The waiter did a double take and smiled toward me, parting those perfectly pink lips. I smiled back, cocking my head backward. I wasn't sure where this would all lead, but I was desperate to go further. I was desperate to touch those lips.

The waiter disappeared inside the café and didn't return. I waited for a few moments and was about to turn and leave when the waiter reappeared, leaving the café from the main entrance. He approached me and I thought the heat would force me to my knees. The waiter hesitated before he spoke, "What's up?"

I told the waiter I was waiting for my family. They were on a ride. The waiter asked if I wanted to "go".

I smirked at the waiter and nodded. I knew where he wanted to take me and I was desperate to be driven. He motioned for me to follow and led me to a nearby restroom. The split-second it took for us both to sneak inside seemed to last forever. Finally, passerby's thinned out and the waiter stepped inside the restroom. I waited a painful fraction of a second before walking in backward behind him. I locked the door. The waiter opened my pants with trembling hands and knelt in front of me. On a hot August evening in California, I fell in love with that waiter. I fell in love with his perfect lips, with his mouth.

I loved Disneyland.

It had been over a year since my father's death. Jean Pierre escorted me to our father's grave. It was a bright yellow morning when we drove through the silent, manicured grounds of the cemetery where my father resides. We found his mother's, my paternal grandmother's grave first. I greeted her with a nod of respect and went on to see my father. My dad's grave was lovely, it overlooked the ocean and was in the company of other celebrities, John Wayne and whoever else. I wonder if my father would get along with John Wayne.

I stood alone at my father's final resting place, while Jean and our mum spoke quietly in the distance. I remembered my father's cruelty. I remembered the abuse and humiliation suffered at his hand. I thought of how suave he was, how he could cloud minds. I thought of how much I looked like him. My face looked exactly like his. I would miss the father he *could* have been. I would miss trying to make him proud and I would miss whatever words he'd never say to me when the world beat me down and I grew cold and fragile. I would miss my father's heavy accent.

Standing at my father's grave I closed my eyes and felt the lament swell within me. I felt all of my regret and sadness rise like rushing water inside my soul and with a heavy sigh I let it all go, I released all of it into the oceanic breeze.

I stood there, taking just a second to remember my dad's face. I took one last look down at my father's grave and said "Bye dad."

We went back to Colorado and reality. Then came sophomore year.

Jeremy and I grew closer, he was my gay best friend. My Advanced Placement art classes continued, drawing and photography, and I loved them. I snuck out of my house as often as possible to adventure with Jeremy and other friends. We met an Austrian schoolmate named Christoph who introduced us to alcohol and amphetamines. I loved the latter; Jeremy gravitated to the former.

I was at school the first time I took speed, I nonchalantly took as much as Christoph had; I didn't want anyone to think it was my first time speeding down that particular racecourse.

I was relieved and a bit disappointed when nothing noticeable happened. I went off to my final class of the day and sat down next to a boy named Jesse. I'd never noticed before how slowly Jesse spoke; his words droned on and on. I looked up at the clock and the seconds were crawling by at a snail's pace. Everyone around me was moving in slow motion. Suddenly I realized my heart was pounding in my chest and I was moving at 1,000 miles an hour. I was a super-speed ingénue, starring in a film directed by God, who was channeling Baz Luhrmann, shot on location in super-real suburbia. I sat in that classroom as my head swam in an infinite sea.

I arrived home after school and retreated to my room, reveling in my newfound toy. I lay on my bed, staring at the ceiling, having hundreds of thousands of thoughts in seconds. Feeling lifetimes come and go as I breathed. A little while later, still in my bedroom, I came down; I crashed like a hijacked luxury liner. I was certain I'd die as my system slowed to a normal, human pace. My metabolism returned to its normal tempo and I hated every agonizing second of it; my lungs ached after their misuse, my skin stopped its frenetic dance, my heart fought to regain its normal beat. My whole body felt like a fish, taken out of water, screaming in dried up agony.

I decided as I fell back to Earth from my brief sojourn in space, that I loved the feeling speed gave me, but not enough to do it regularly after the violent crash I had just experienced.

Jeremy and I shared grand adventures; sneaking into clubs, ditching school for afternoon shopping sprees and throwing private dance parties at his house while unsupervised. We left school one morning for Denver intent on purchasing Madonna's book Sex. Jeremy and I were waiting for the shops on the 16th Street Mall to open in the lobby of a luxury hotel, when a band of stupidly grinning teenagers pounced on us. The other teens were stalking the band U2, who were in town for a show and staying in the hotel. Jeremy and I went with the teens to the penthouses, where we liberated bottles of wine from discarded room service trays.

As we prepared to leave the hotel and travel back to Golden, we saw limousines pull up to the side entrance. Jeremy and I watched as the band exited the hotel and got into the waiting vehicles, the kids we had met in the lobby were waiting in a crowd across from us. The band's guitarist waved to the assembled fans and thanked them for coming out, while apologizing for not having the time to sign anything.

Had thought of it I would've thanked him for the wine.

That day I realized celebrity was a veneer. Fame was all a big sham. Up close, a few feet away, these guys were nothing special. They were middle-aged men with crow's feet around their eyes, dressed too young for their age. "Fame" was there for the taking by anyone smart, brave, stupid, needy or hungry enough to put themselves out for public consumption. Furthermore, page after page of Madonna's book proved that some people were *so* hungry for fame; they'd *utterly* debase themselves.

I may have missed a day of school, but I learned invaluable lessons.

I spent the rest of sophomore year dreaming violet dreams; I imagined the perfect lover and kept trying to fill the vacant role with the candidates closest to me. I had visions of orchestrating the ideal love scene, I'd be surrounded by fields of lilies and drown in teenage passion. There were problems casting the role, no ingénue in my direct sphere of influence was worthy of the part.

I went to school as often as I could stand it and went wild as often as my friends, the law and social convention would allow. The first flowers of spring began to appear and the temperatures grew warmer, like my blood. I found that the hotter it was *outside*, the hotter I became *inside*. I could feel heat radiate in my head, like I was afflicted with some terrible fever that began at my core and radiated outward, devouring everything in its path. If the world around me were to burn, surely my mind would collapse in feverous ruin.

I was lying on a girl's chest between classes, as she reclined in an outdoor common area. I began to playfully tug at the girl's shirt with my teeth. Like most animals, when they get something in their teeth, they can't surrender. I was no different. I was swept up by the crude, feral sensation. I bit down hard on the shirt and began to violently thrash my head from side to side. As my senses cleared I realized someone was screaming, a girl was screaming. I realized I hadn't had the girl's shirt in my mouth at all, but her skin.

I apologized profusely and walked the girl to the nurse's station. I felt awkward and silly; I was just having fun. I hadn't meant to hurt her. The girl's family tried to file charges against me, my mum had to deliver me to the local police station for questioning. After a lengthy interview with an understanding police officer and some explanations of the girl's character and lifestyle, it was decided no charges would be pursued.

The moral of the story is, don't let a monster lay on your chest.

Vampires bite, stupid.

After the school year ended, Jeremy's family was moving back to
Montana, where they originated. The last time I saw Jeremy before he was
to leave, we spent the day shopping downtown for clothes at perpetually
cutting edge boutiques, Fashionation and Imi Jimi, and vintage records
at Wax Trax. In the afternoon we separated to go home and choose our
costumes for the night. Then around 10 pm, cause nobody good goes out
before 10, we met up and drove into the city. Jeremy and I spent hours on
the dance floor at Rock Island as huge video screens showed wild footage
behind us. We'd dance just a little bit harder when someone beautiful
began moving toward us on the crowded stage. That last night of well-
intended innocence with Jeremy was amazing. We were best friends
moving to the same beat and having a blast. We were brothers dancing till
the end of the world.

Chapter 8: THE LOST YEARS PART ONE:
WALKING IN PERPETUAL FLAMES, DANCING ON GLASS AND THE FIRST DEATH

Junior year began and my best friend was gone, I cared very little about the day-to-day life of an 11th grader. I excelled in my studio art classes and found myself drafted into Advanced Placement History and English courses. I wasn't at all interested in school, least of all history and English. I was living for the nighttime, dance clubs and secret rendezvous. In retrospect, this was a huge mistake.

I was obsessed with music; I'd score my life like a film, setting each scene with the appropriate songs. I loved the seemingly directionless rebellion of punk and its awkward masculine energy. I loved the tragic romance and petulant angst of goth. I loved the mechanical aggression of industrial. I adored the danceable hedonism of disco. I worshipped soul, while classic freestyle and funk could always make my spirit move, even if my body was standing still.

11th grade would be my last. Eventually, I just stopped going to school.

I would attend school, throwing myself into art and photography, but I'd sleep walk through my other classes. I'd get home and barricade myself in my room till sundown, when I'd go wild. After a night out I'd return home with enough time to sleep for a few hours, shower and rush off to school. My life was an ill-advised thrill ride of epic proportions.

Christoph and I took a couple of girls to Ground Zero on Halloween night. Ground Zero was literally an underground alternative club. It was a black, subterranean lair of unrepentant hedonism, located under the streets of Boulder. Halloween fell on a Sunday that year and Sunday's were among the most popular at Ground Zero, the most crowded. Add Halloween to the Sunday night mystique and you had an evening pregnant with possibilities. We sped down Highway 93, a gravely scenic and foreboding stretch of quiet shadows and nothing, arriving at the club after 10pm. I noticed a blonde punk rocker beneath me, while I danced on the highest tier of the dance floor. He looked tough and sinewy, the sleeves were cut off his faded t-shirt and he wore engineering boots. He was baby-faced, blonde and blue eyed. I watched him dance and admired his angelic beauty.

I had a nightmare that night. I was walking through a deserted post-apocalyptic city, not another soul was present. Suddenly a shadow moved across the ground. I looked up to see the punk rocker from the club, he had angel's wings, but they were mechanical and decrepit, like an animatronic after the artificial skin had been removed. The angel lowered himself to the ground and stood before me, I knelt in his presence. The angel thrust a flaming sword through my chest and I could feel my heart turning to ash. Life deserted my body, I looked into the angel's eyes and whispered, "I love you."

I woke up in the early morning hours of November 1st. It was cold in my bedroom and I couldn't breathe. I had just enough time to rise and dress for a long day of school.

My art teacher encouraged me to attend a national portfolio review event held in Denver. I met representatives from schools in New York and San Francisco, both offered me incentives to attend and invited my mum and I to their campuses. I refused both. I knew I was a terrible student and my life expectancy would surely plummet in so decedent a city.

I began going to Ground Zero five nights a week, Wednesday through Monday. The first night I returned after Halloween, my Austrian friend Christoph, who also frequented the club, introduced me to the blonde punk rocker; he was a friend of Christoph's. The punk rocker's name was Coby; a fittingly pedestrian appellation. Raised in the low-income wilds of suburbia, Coby was the personification of young

American trash. Coby was made of punk rock snarls and a rebellious mentality, but he lacked the intellect and vocabulary required to actually subvert anything. Coby did have a certain hot, white trash mystique about him and it was enthralling.

Christoph and Coby showed up on my doorstep one school night and asked if I wanted to go driving with them; they didn't know where we'd go, but we were gonna stay out good and late. I agreed. We drove around aimlessly in Christoph's MR2, a gift from his father. Coby had to sit on my lap. The three of us ended up at Muddy's, a bohemian coffee house catering to the same youthful scary monsters that haunted my favorite parts of the city. We each took a handful of Black Beauties, amphetamines, from Christoph; he always had drugs on him, like a pharmacist in a long black coat. Coby didn't want to return to what he said was a dysfunctional home that night and begged me to let him stay with me. I eventually relented and agreed to a slumber party.

Coby was nothing like the kids I was used to; he was rough and street, he had homemade tattoos and an energy that made me want to devour him. Coby was rough trade; he was punk rock trash with a handsome, boyish face and a perfectly pale body. I was immediately and dangerously attracted to him. I had to get him alone. I snuck Coby into my house and we crept upstairs to my bedroom. I told him I felt guilty having him sleep alone on the floor, so I joined him.

The next day Coby came to school with me, we counted down the long hours of the day together, till Christoph came to pick Coby up and take him home.

Easter was the following weekend; Christoph and I hung out the afternoon of Good Friday. We sped through the streets of Denver, listening to music too loudly and ranting about other kids in the club scene. I bought a pair of black patent Doc Martens, we planned to go to Ground Zero that night for some typical rebellion; slamming into other kids, posing and dancing.

We walked into Ground Zero and the club was seething with tension, everyone was in a frenzied mood. The music was fast and dangerous. The lights throbbed like a beating heart; smoke machines obscured your identity enough that you could be anyone. I saw Coby across the club; I could feel his eyes following me, burning me with their intensity.

I was so stupidly naïve. Coby's eyes told the story; he was angry, jealous, confused and about to unleash absolute chaos.

Coby had been telling everyone who would listen that we had sex, he claimed I seduced him the night he stayed with me. We hadn't and I didn't. I was impossibly attracted to Coby, but nothing happened between us. That night at my house, Coby took his shirt off for bed, he could tell I was watching him with hungry eyes and he teased me. He took a pair of domination cuffs from my vanity and bound my hands behind my back, then caressed his chest. That was the extent of our tryst. He teased me. There was no contact between us. Coby's tale escalated to the point where he was telling everyone in the club I had raped him.

I was horrified and fled the club in shame; I physically felt every whisper as I passed through the club. I felt every judgmental gaze rake across my soul like talons against raw flesh. The following night Christoph called to tell me the management of Ground Zero had banned me; I could never go back. I had been a rising name on the scene and Coby had destroyed my reputation in one, devastating swoop.

I was ready to die that night. Like a petulant child, I was ready to destroy myself rather than let someone, anyone get the best of me. My mind raced, my mind raged. I would rather die than allow Coby, this commoner, this trash, to debase my name and reputation. I sat alone in my family's living room, in darkness and silence.

My family never threw out prescriptions; half full bottles were readily available. In the short moments before dawn, when the night is at it's darkest, when goodness is afraid to come out and when light simply surrenders to shadow and anything can happen, I swallowed a heaping handful of drugs. I swallowed a mix of painkillers, antidepressants and barbiturates that I was confident would prove lethal.

My body began to feel heavy and leaden, it was hard to move and harder to think. Everything looked gray. I felt so tired, like a lifetime had passed since I last slept. I could see the sun rising in the East; it filled the room with warm, rust colored light. As the sun rose in the sky, the light grew warmer and cleaner.

A tiny, frail voice in the back of my mouth demanded, "Live."

I stumbled to the front door and fumbled with the locks, I crawled outside across the cold concrete of our front step and into the damp, dewy grass. I stared into the sun and was reborn. I forced myself to vomit and wretched as half-digested pill after pill flowed from my mouth in a sick waterfall of bile. My stomach and chest ached from misuse, my arms and legs hurt. My head throbbed and my eyes struggled in the bright new day's sun.

I was alive. I had faced death and found it wanting.

That was my first death.

I received a call the following weekend from the manager of Ground Zero; he asked were I had been, I told him I'd heard I was banned from the club. The manager laughed and said everyone knew Coby was a pathological liar. Coby had only succeeded in perpetuating my rapidly growing infamy.

Weeks later I ran into Coby at a birthday party. After a teenage orgy in the basement, which Coby did not participate in, and after conferring with the hostess, I held Coby at gunpoint until he confessed his lie. A room full of partygoers overheard Coby's admission and I was the victor.

Coby taught me one thing; I would have to attempt to carefully measure my passion and intensity in future, lest it destroy me.

Chapter 9: UNNATURAL MOVEMENTS OF THE FLESH

Sex was a weapon. Not like a handgun, but a knife, something sleek and sharp. I could stab right to someone's heart if I needed to, or I could cut away at someone's life by severing their connection to the person they loved. Their boyfriend. Girlfriend. Husband. Wife. Whatever.

I had numerous affairs, a 21-year-old queen of the goth scene named Stephanie, a rivet head named Travis. None of them lasted; my attraction usually ended the second I ejaculated on or in them.

Stephanie was an older girl who convinced herself she loved me. Our liaison was doomed from the start, she was the coolest girl in the scene and I needed a new high profile relationship to recover from Coby. Later I heard Stephanie died of a drug overdose, but that would happen years into a veiled future. Stephanie and I were at Ground Zero one Saturday night when I met a boy name Nelse.

I had seen Nelse before, our eyes locked on the dance floor, forcing our minds to play a film of mutual teenage passion. Nelse looked expensive and successful; Coby had been punk rock and leather, he was the Misfits. Nelse was perfectly tailored; he was New Order and the Pet Shop Boys. Nelse had large, sensitive eyes and pouty lips; I was just a little taller than him.

I ran into Nelse in a dark hallway that led to the bathrooms. We tried to speak to each other, but the furious music made it impossible to hear. I pulled Nelse into an alcove that was once a phone booth. The phone had long ago been vandalized beyond repair; nobody that deep in the cavernous heart of Ground Zero would be calling the outside world. Nelse and I moved toward one another as we spoke, so we could hear over the loud music. I brought my mouth to his ear, just above his neck. I could see Nelse's pulse dancing in his veins; I could smell his cologne. I could feel the heat radiating off his skin. Nelse moved to respond to what I had said, his lips a treacherous few inches from my own ear. Nelse's mouth grazed my neck as he spoke.

I knew Stephanie and her friends would be looking for me, so I turned to Nelse and said, "Let's get out of here."

"Yeah." Nelse responded with a smile.

Nelse and I ran from the club and we sped up the winding mountain road atop Lookout Mountain in Golden. Nelse's car stopped at a steep overlook, we sat in the car and spoke softly. Neither of us could catch our breath. Nelse and I ran out of words moments after we parked. We turned toward one another and shared a perfect kiss, that kiss held the promise of first love. We devoured each other.

By the end of that first night we told each other "I love you."

I was 17 and in love. For three months, which for a young man that age is a lifetime, I was faithful to Nelse, until one night when I was too sick with a cold to attend a party with him. The host was a young lad I'd slept with and discarded, so I assumed I wouldn't have been welcome anyway. A rumor got back to me that Nelse had been flirting with another guy. I called Nelse the next day and told him we were over. I loved Nelse, but I couldn't allow my image to be jeopardized. I couldn't be seen forgiving a lover with a straying hand. It didn't matter whether or not the rumor was true.

One of the first tattoos I received was an anatomic heart with a ribbon flowing around it, carrying Nelse's name. I wanted to remember those urgent, perfect 90 days.

Chapter 10: THE LOST YEARS PART TWO:
IN THE VALLEY OF THE DOLLS THROUGH THE VELVET SHADOW OF DEATH

I hid out in seclusion, recuperating in the wilds of Golden from the burns I'd suffered. My love for Nelse flared hot and intense, my heart was scarred and tender, but ashes are all that's left in the wake of a burned out fire.

I began working at a video store in the local mall, it was my first taste of normal adolescence and it wouldn't last. I was never on time. I hated following orders. I met a girl named Wendy while on the job; she was the store's assistant manager and quickly showed a romantic interest in me. I didn't intend to reciprocate those feelings, but I needed an ally and Wendy was immediately and utterly devoted to me. Wendy would clock me in when my shift was to start, while I was still across town and en route.

Wendy was a pretty girl, but she was tough, a typical tomboy; she was overprotective to the point of suffocating me. I needed to be protected, if not from my numerous suitors, then certainly from myself.

Wendy snuck me into my first gay club; it was intimidating for a 17 year old. The Compound was a rough trade bar filled with shirtless daddies, muscle heads and twinks. I loved it. I'd steal champagne from my family's wine rack, Wendy and I would sip the bubbly straight from the bottle while we sped into the city, toward bars we weren't old enough to get into and shouldn't have been in.

Wendy and I had planned to dance at an all-ages gay club; clearly we'd need some champagne to survive the company of that many gyrating teenagers. We never hung out with teenagers outside of the punk or goth

43

scene. We stopped at Cheesman Park, renowned for it's drug dealing, gay prostitution and cruising; it was late in the evening. I had planned to enjoy the bubbly and then replace the cork, hoping no one at home would notice the mysteriously empty bottle. The cork shot out across the grass like a rocket with a deliciously effervescent jet stream. The park was dark and creepy, filled with lurkers and lecherous men. I made Wendy crawl around on all fours among the dope dealers and whores, till she found the cork.

Jacques and I didn't get along as teens, we were from different worlds; he wanted to be some girl's boyfriend and eventual husband, I wanted to take the world to bed and dance my ass off. Jacques was happy to be a face in the crowd, surrounded by suburban skaters. I wanted to be a star and in the spotlight. We eventually reconciled and began spending time together, we'd organize large expeditions to Ground Zero for retro Sunday nights. Slowly Jacques and I outgrew childhood differences and began to care about each other; soon we were devoted siblings.

Golden had an annual summertime parade and festival honoring Buffalo Bill Cody; I usually went with my family. Thea and I were walking back to her car after the festivities when we saw a car plow through a crowd of spectators, we watched as bodies were thrown over the hood of the car as it bore into the innocent crowd like a wheat thresher. Thea and I both ran to help, offering what assistance we could till emergency services arrived. I felt helpless and horrified, I was ashamed that I couldn't do more; I wanted to rewind the clock and warn the grandmothers and children out of the car's path.

Ground Zero closed its doors that fall, on Halloween night. I had spent countless hours in that club and a small chapter of my youth ended with its passing. I was dangerously underweight and taking amphetamines with increasing frequency. All the scene kids found a new place to haunt, a club called Synergy, a cavernous playground in the imposing, low rent warehouse district of Denver.

My art was juried into a show, a statewide exhibition of artists. It was a big accomplishment for a young man who had not yet turned 18. I didn't care; my life was about hedonism, pills, music and street fashion.

I had blossomed into a black-plastic peacock, confident and cocky, swaggering and posing. I loved my appearance and my hard-to-believe, angular face. I began getting tattooed, covering my arms with images that signified pivotal moments I'd survived. I reveled in my appearance, that and my charm allowed me to get away with almost anything. With a bit of suave charisma, I could acquire nearly anything I wanted. I had finally grown to love being Kristian, but the road to that point had been long and arduous. Everyday was a circus and I put myself in the center ring, every evening was a treacherously dilapidated carnival ride.

Unbeknownst to me at the time, my future would be fraught with danger and violence, due to no one but myself. Nights would start out innocently but devolve into burning dumpsters, vandalized cars and irresponsible sex in alleys.

My mum had left town for a week, Jacques and I were staying alone in our home. I was filled with restless energy, it was late at night and the walls were closing in on me. I took a skateboard from Jacques' room and wondered the twilight streets of my neighborhood. I passed safe houses, with pedestrian families locked up tight inside. I passed my elementary school, a place I'd grown to hate. The summer breeze cooled my skin as I sped through the streets, but I was still burning up inside.

I stopped at a convenience store on the edge of town; it was deserted except for the young clerk inside. The clerk was named Kevin; he had gone to elementary school with me but disappeared after exposing himself to a girl in our class. One day Kevin had approached me in the schoolyard and ground his pelvis into mine, he said, "Let's piss on each other." I remember asking myself if Kevin was coming on to me. We were in first grade.

I walked through the gas station aimlessly, glancing up at Kevin through heavily lidded eyes. Kevin was hot in a thuggish, white-boy capacity; he had dark blonde hair, slicked back on top and a cute face. Kevin asked me if I needed anything, I looked up into his eyes and offered an unspoken answer. Kevin led me into the backroom; he asked if I were clean because he had a wife and baby at home. I confirmed my immaculate status and Kevin went down on me. A week later I went back and fucked Kevin, I bent him over the sink in the employee bathroom. Kevin wasn't at the gas station the next time Wendy and I stopped in before clubbing.

I met a lad named Flower at Synergy. Flower was tall and imposing, masculine and tattooed, just like me. We danced on the podiums above the rest of the crowd. Flower and I competed for the same attention. I disliked him at first, Flower copied my style; he stole the way I danced, the way I dressed, even the smeared eyeliner I was wearing at the time. Flower had no identity of his own, so he borrowed mine. Flower stole a portion of my glow and I hated him for it, but I did need a second in command, and he was obviously a follower. I brought Flower into my inner circle. I knew he was a derivative sycophant, but I needed a male friend who would follow orders.

That era was one of the most dangerous and certainly the angriest I'd experienced. My spirit was an inexhaustible atomic furnace of rage. I was torn between my hatred for myself and the entire world.

A small club in Denver closed their doors in my honor; allowing me to throw a private, invite only Halloween party. I gave out custom-made voodoo dolls, designed to resemble each guest. One of Jacques' friends brought a girl, uninvited and unwanted. Her name was Hannah.

Hannah was a beautiful 19-year-old stripper; her heart was fractured into innumerable pieces, like a broken mirror. I loved looking at her and seeing my reflection, repeated countless times on her shattered soul.

I began spending every night and most days with Hannah, we became addicted to each other, I was falling in love with her. Hannah seemed to be drawn to my destructive side, she wanted it; she embraced it. The hotter I burned, the more Hannah seemed to want me, a self-perpetuating cycle of rock star dysfunction. I was descending further and further into violent self-indulgence and Hannah seemed to love it. I loved her, so I let myself slip away.

I hate to remember these years.

Flower and I made out and fellated each other in the bathroom of a theater after attending the Denver premiere of a David Lynch film; Hannah was waiting outside. I knew I was hurting her, but she loved me when I was wild. I was breaking Hannah's heart, but I told myself she wanted it.

The scene kids discovered and exploited a new club called the Snake Pit, a multi-roomed temple of beats, booze and lust. I met an Asian goth boy named D' at a tiny dive club whose name I can't remember. I thought D' was gay, he was effeminate and he wore dated make-up and plastic dresses with his combat boots and fishnet hose. D' epitomized everything I thought was passé, everything I hated about the gothic-industrial scene. My initial assumption was wrong, D' wasn't gay, he just had a strong lisp and wore too much eyeliner.

D' was a footnote at the time, just another face at the club. He'd eventually grow to become a substantial force in my life, but that was all for another day.

HANNAH.
Photo by Christopher Schadenfreude

Chapter 11: THE LOST YEARS PART THREE: THE SECOND, THIRD AND FOURTH DEATH

I continued to behave monstrously, there are so many stories I could recount here, but I'm afraid to. I don't want memory to take me down a path I've worked hard to move beyond, to recover from.

Hannah and I were social royalty; pedestrians would compliment us on how we complimented each other, they'd tell us how good we looked together. Hannah's stripper friends threw a party; she and I attended. I was already intoxicated when we arrived. I locked myself in the bathroom and ingested a staggering amount of weapons-grade narcotics. My head was swimming but I continued to take more drugs. I'd been experimenting with some dangerous substances; my drug use would reach a crescendo that night. I had taken a crippling cocktail of narcotics and alcohol, suddenly my body refused to obey me.

I was sitting in a dimly lit room, on a stripper's bed, while she and her friends smoked pot from a hookah. My mind functioned perfectly, but the mental connection between my mind and body was abruptly severed. My limbs refused to move. I could barely speak. I was overdosing on a mixture of amphetamines, vodka and heroin. I panicked, the girls left the room but I couldn't follow. I couldn't move. I was sweating profusely, but I was shivering. My skin was gray.

Eventually Hannah came to search for me, she found me in a crumpled, frustrated heap. Hannah knelt beside me; through sheer force of will my mind convinced my arms to obey my commands, but just barely. I roughly grabbed Hannah and pulled her close to me. I could hardly speak, but I was able to hiss my words at her.

I whispered sweet, threatening slurs in Hannah's ear through gnashed teeth and pulled her closer to me, ever closer. I could smell her skin, soft and sweet and delicate. I held her closer; both of my hands were gripping Hannah's upper arms tightly. Hannah tried to pull away and I squeezed, tightening my already uncomfortable grip on her arms.

"You're hurting me!" Hannah said and jerked her body away from mine, once more abandoning me in the dark room; she turned to look at me as she left. I peered up at her from under my brow, my chin lowered against my chest.

I wanted Hannah's kiss to revive me, just like a fairytale princess. I wanted her love to bring me back to life, instead I held her too tightly and she slipped away.

Finally my mind shut down, everything went gray. Blissful oblivion. Everything just stopped, including my breathing. That was my second death. I remember being put in the bathtub and then hearing the strippers discuss whether or not to throw me in the swimming pool in an attempt to revive me.

I regained consciousness in my bed, the sun was up and I had no idea what day it was. I was cold.

Thank God for perpetual resurrection, especially for the undeserving.

My life became a carousel and I was the main attraction, I was the dilapidated show pony everyone wanted to ride. Every night degenerated into a cinematic, sin-o-matic debacle of drugs, lust, music and often violence. I coerced Hannah into masturbating with the neck of a tequila bottle in a room full of young men; she was playing truth or dare with my friends and I. I hate tequila. I trashed a rival's car, stomping on the roof, kicking the doors in and spitting on the windows. These were my nights.

One Friday night we were dancing at a goth club with the other baby bats. Hannah and I carved our initials into a boy's arm with a razor blade. Hannah cut "HN" deeply in to his soft flesh; she was using my last name. Hannah cut so deep we could see the pink fat under the boy's skin

49

spilling out from the wound like waves made of meat.

Good lord.

One's past can lead them down such traumatizing and tragic paths, can't it?

To be honest, I'm glad *this* Kristian died.

Hannah and I chose baby names for the child we'd have; my son's name was going to be Bela Louis. After my dad and Bela Lugosi, an actor I revered, my two favorite vampires. My son was going to be creative and smart; he'd look just like me. After Bela Louis was born I'd realize how stupid and immature I had been. I'd turn over a new leaf to give my son the kind of father he deserved. I'd give my son the kind of father *I* deserved. Bela Louis was going to be sensitive and empathic, the kind of child that would make you strive to be the best role model possible. My son was going to save my life, and I'd spend the rest of my life working hard, trying my best to live up to being this amazing little boy's father.

My son was going to be amazing.

He was going to be *amazing*.

Hannah told me that if she ever became pregnant, she'd flee, she'd run and hide from my family. Fate had other ideas. Hannah would never get the chance.

I trashed Hannah's apartment during a party and no one stopped me, the other guests observed at best and encouraged at worst. I punched ceramic masks from her wall and shattered the glass of framed pictures as I passed. A mutual friend had invited his beautiful best friend, a recently paroled rockabilly named Larry. Larry was square jawed and dangerous, he was tough and tattooed and coifed. Sexual energy rose off of Larry's skin like steam emanating from hot pavement. Larry was also an intravenous drug user and HIV positive.

After I'd destroyed the interior of Hannah's apartment, Larry and I locked ourselves in her bathroom and kissed. I was out of control and flirting with grave danger. I bit Larry's lip, breaking the skin and could taste the sick copper-crimson of disease flow into my mouth. Larry pushed me away and grabbed my face, scolding me. I laughed at him.

My third death.

Life continued to spiral downward in the following weeks, I spent every available moment with Hannah, pulling her close and then smashing her down and pushing her away; she seemed to love it. The worse I became, the bigger the monster I was, the more she clung to me. Until…

Hannah began to have anxiety attacks, once suffering an attack so severe while we were driving that she swerved us off the road and had to get out of the car, she couldn't breathe. I was watching the girl I loved die and I laughed at her. Soon Hannah refused to see me and eventually fled to California to escape me. The end.

In truth, I hate the man I was then and I'm glad he wouldn't survive.

I was hired as a burlesque dancer at a big budget Halloween attraction called Brutal Planet. The venue took up a city block and was perfectly staged to look like a futuristic city gone apocalyptic. My first night on stage, in a frenzy, I broke an empty beer bottle and slashed the sharp glass across my chest. In the strobing red light of the stage and with the crowd screaming in excitement, I didn't notice how bad the wound was. The song I was dancing to came to an end and I went backstage. Blood ran down my chest, into the waistband of my tight vinyl pants, into my white Calvin Klein briefs. There was so much blood.

I poured peroxide from a first aid kit over my chest, closed the deep gash as best I could with small, white butterfly bandages and took the stage again as soon as my intro boomed through the venue. The audience roared with applause when I tore my shirt open to reveal my lacerated chest, I was reveling in the audience's horrified approval. I repeated the routine again, over and over, cutting my chest open countless times throughout the duration of the show.

I didn't wound myself for any great emotional release, I didn't do it because I was sad or felt guilty. I cut myself open over and over again, night after night because the audience loved it. I did it all for the money.

That show, Brutal Planet, did seem to help me exorcise the demons that were haunting me. I had been filled with aggression and frustration and hate. That show and its exhausting, non-stop schedule of performances ran the engine in my spirit to death. By the time the show ended I was no longer as angry as I had been, I was just severely lacerated and tired. That show and my behavior then was one long, repetitious death. I was empty and exhausted and ready for another resurrection.

A 21st Century Marquis DeSade
Photo by Christopher Schadenfreude

Chapter 12: ORBITAL RESURRECTION (INTERLUDE)

I was a blank slate, newly cleansed and reborn. I hid out for months, away from nightclubs and drugs and trouble. I was an alien who had crash-landed and was now stranded on Earth. The future stretched out before me like an infinite highway.

I knew it had been a mistake to leave school; I had wasted countless hours twisting my body to heavy dance beats and survived the nighttime warzone of America's underground youth, but hadn't done something so simple as graduate high school. I decided I would alleviate this. One day I decided I'd take the General Educational Development tests, the GED. I didn't study; I didn't so much as open a book. I didn't prepare. I just arrived at a test facility one day and took the tests in a single sitting. The tests took me a little over 90 minutes to complete and I scored just above the national average.

I wonder how well I'd have done if I tried, if I'd studied or exerted myself.

I turned 21 that summer and Jeremy moved back to Denver, I was finally reunited with my best friend. I had such stories to tell Jeremy, we resumed our friendship as if not a single second had passed.

Jeremy's arrival made going to clubs fun again, Wendy would drive us to the Snake Pit or the Church, an actual decommissioned church, complete with archaic atmosphere and gothic architecture. Jeremy and Wendy immediately disliked each other, they were both overprotective of me and each felt they were my "best friend". Jeremy had the seniority and the upper hand; he and I had never for a single second been any more than platonic brothers-in-arms. Wendy entertained foolish notions of falling in love with me, that wasn't what I needed from a friend.

I ran into D', the surprisingly straight, faggy goth guy at the Snake Pit, he mentioned he was looking to start a band. I had always felt like a star, even if no one else saw my potential, and had always wanted to sing. We agreed to meet later to discuss collaborating musically; I knew our paths were linked from that moment on. D' became a close friend; I would hang out at the apartment he shared with his awful girlfriend and work on ideas for music, afterward we'd go club hopping. Jeremy loved the creative, artistic environment I lived in. We were all tough wanna-be rock stars.

D's girlfriend was a trite and overpowering personality named Jolene, she had no discernable talent for anything, but wanted to critique everything. I hated spending any amount of time with her, she resented anything D' would or could accomplish without her. I swallowed my venom for Jolene by reasoning that I had more to gain by collaborating with D' than I lost by fraternizing with her.

D' and I began writing songs together almost immediately, I christened our collaboration Heroin; if we were ever to play a show, that's the name we'd use. We had little money and scarce resources, but we had unstoppable ambition and creativity. D' had a crude home studio and we'd create music using whatever guerilla tactics were necessary. A pair of women's hose and a twisted metal clothes hanger became a filter to sing through, a closet became a vocal booth.

Jeremy and I began to strut and posture through Denver's club scene, earning an often well-deserved negative reputation. D' soon joined us. We were dangerous boys; we'd feed off of each other's bravado. The three of us went to a gay club one night after working in the studio. While D', Jeremy and I stood at the urinals in the men's room, a drunken patron tried to flirt with me. I turned toward the drunk and let loose a heavy flow of warm urine that flowed down his midsection and legs. D' and Jeremy roared with laughter, a typical night out with my boys.

D' and I recorded demos and sent them to a list of record companies. We were so young and naïve, we thought the rough ideas we'd patched together were good enough to land us a record deal; we were over confidant. The night once again became my kingdom and I was a benevolent and majestic emperor, I let the night air caress my body like the fingers of the perfect lover. I danced so hard my chest hurt, up on podiums so the entire club could see me. I searched the city for a brand new love, to replace the ones I'd discarded or broken.

Everything was a heady, cinematic adventure.

We were all antiheroes. We were young. We were brave. We were brilliant.

Chapter 13: THE LONGEST SILENT NIGHT

Jacques and I were best friends, but we hated each other sometimes. We spent our childhood clinging to each other in the turbulent sea that was our family; it wasn't easy to be a child in that environment and outsiders would never understand like a brother. When we weren't clinging to one another, we were fighting. He broke my Darth Vader action figure's head off. I burned his Han Solo till he was unrecognizable.

Jacques and I spent our teens in different worlds; we grew apart as we evolved into young men, my life was too different from his. We'd grown apart. We ignored each other on a good day and fist fought like street hoods on bad days. It wasn't till the sun set on our adolescence that we rallied back toward each other. Slowly we built a sophisticated relationship, we'd bond over comic books or music. I was a night person; Jacques was a morning person. He was more handsome; I was smarter. He was an instinctive fighter; I wanted to be a lover.

Jacques would wake up hours before me on Sundays; I'd have been out all night the evening before. He'd patiently wait for me to clean up and dress and we'd head out for the day, shopping, seeing shows, having lunch, and browsing comic shops. We spent every Sunday together. Jacques and I made a formidable duo; we were both young, handsome men. Jacques possessed a misplaced and disarming social awkwardness that made him more appealing and approachable to the masses. I knew I was charismatic and used it to my advantage at every opportunity. Jacques and I were very different sides of the same coin.

JACQUES AND I, I'M THE BUNNY.
Photo by Victoria Coco

I went out one Friday night with Wendy and Jeremy; it was a monumental effort to force the two of them to behave civilly toward one another. Jeremy hated Wendy's forked, passive-aggressive tongue. Our evening was epic; we drank Stolichnaya straight from the bottle on the drive into the city. Jeremy and I ran around a crowded club, while Wendy seethed at our table. I met a handsome British rogue named Albert; we pawed each other hungrily in the men's room. Albert and I consumed one another in a stall while my friends wondered where I was; he gave me a key to his hotel room. I intended to rendezvous with Albert and his pale, toned body and sea green eyes as soon as I divested myself of Jeremy and Wendy.

I returned home after closing Proteus, the club we'd gone to. I could hear the phone ringing from outside as I walked up the driveway. My mind was still swimming in vodka cocktails. I opened the door and answered the phone; it was my mum. She had been calling over and over for hours, waiting till I returned home.

My mum told me not to go in the bathroom, so of course that was the first thing I did. I swung the door open and the smell from the bathtub washed over me like a wave, I could smell the familiar sick, wet crimson-copper of blood. I could smell a *lot* of blood. I flicked the light on and scanned the room frantically. The bathroom looked like a crime scene. I asked my mother what had happened; she said Jacques cut his wrists. Jacques did this to himself over a girl.

I needed to get to the hospital, Jacques was still alive and under suicide watch in the ER. I ran upstairs to change clothes. I couldn't go see my brother in the clothes I'd worn clubbing. My bedroom door wouldn't open, I tried to force it, but it refused to open. I punched my fist through the door, but couldn't withdraw my hand after it smashed through to the other side. I punched the door with my other hand, till both fists were a flurry of splinters and rage. My bedroom door was reduced to broken wreckage. I was confused and frustrated and I felt helpless. For the first time since I was a small child, I cried.

I thought we'd become so strong, I couldn't rationalize how Jacques could do such a thing. Over a girl.

I finally made it to the hospital and made my way to Jacques. Our siblings converged one by one. My entire family pulled together to save Jacques from his dangerously theatrical attempt to get a girl's attention.

That night in the hospital Jacques asked me to get home before any of the other siblings. He asked me to find the notes he'd left and destroy them before our mum could read them. I agreed. I sped home and found the notes Jacques referred to; there were two, one addressed to our mum and one addressed to me. I opened the small folded squares one by one and my throat felt as dry as a desert. I read mum's note first. He apologized. Then I read my note from Jacques, the note he intended to be our final communication. I don't remember most of what it said.

I only remember the last line; he wrote, "Thanks for being my best friend."

My brother.

I did as Jacques requested and burned the notes before anyone else could see them.

That event, Jacques' near death, was one of the most visceral and frustrating moments of my life. I couldn't coldly fix everything. I couldn't control any of it. I felt crippled and helpless.

I tried to go out with Wendy and Jeremy; we went to the Church and Millennium, a rich new club in Boulder. I tried to dance off my worries; I wanted to exorcise my demons with driving drums and throbbing bass. I was at the Snake Pit with Wendy, dancing on a podium, when a thuggy Irish guy approached me; looking like he'd walked right out of Boston, the guy was wearing sagged pants and a backwards baseball cap, he was pale and freckled. The white boy had broad shoulders and a tough, round face, he waited patiently till the song I was dancing to ended and extended his hand to me as I climbed down. It was then that I recognized him, the Irish guy was a kid named Shamus from Golden High.

Shamus was a straight catholic boy who had a real problem with Jeremy and I. In school Shamus was a typical nobody, a pedestrian who wanted to protect his masculinity at all costs. Jeremy and I were a threat to heterosexuality everywhere; we threatened the very fabric of teenage life and the wholesome values in Golden. Shamus took every opportunity to call us faggots or shout spiteful slurs at us as we walked through the halls. Shamus spit at us. Literally.

Now, the Irish boy was here at the Snake Pit, offering me his hand. Shamus asked me to walk outside with him and I complied. Life had made me tough enough to fight an Irish catholic one on one. Besides, by then Shamus looked like everybody I had gone to school with: tired and spent. Once we got outside, Shamus seemed harmless, defenseless and sincere. Shamus' big, green eyes filled with emotion, he looked like the freakishly large-eyed angels drawn on greeting cards. Shamus spoke to me in a soft, repentant tone, he apologized for everything he'd ever said or done to me. Shamus said he'd learned about life since high school and knew how wrong he was. Shamus said he was sorry and that he wanted to be friends. Shamus offered to buy me a drink.

My brother had just tried to kill himself and I wasn't feeling diplomatic. I wasn't interested in being generously forgiving. I wasn't ready to absolve Shamus and I wasn't going to share a drink with a newly evolved catholic. Shamus didn't matter to me, nor did his newfound enlightenment. I didn't need or want anyone's approval to live my life. Thoughts like Shamus' epitomized obsolescence; I was the future. Shamus would only receive indifference.

I patted Shamus' shoulder as I walked past him and told him, "No, thank you."

Sorry Shamus. But, I *am* glad you saw the light.

SAVE US FROM THESE KNIGHTS OF SUBURBIA
Photo by Victoria Coco

College Graduate, with Honors and Against All Odds

Photo by Alexander Nevermind

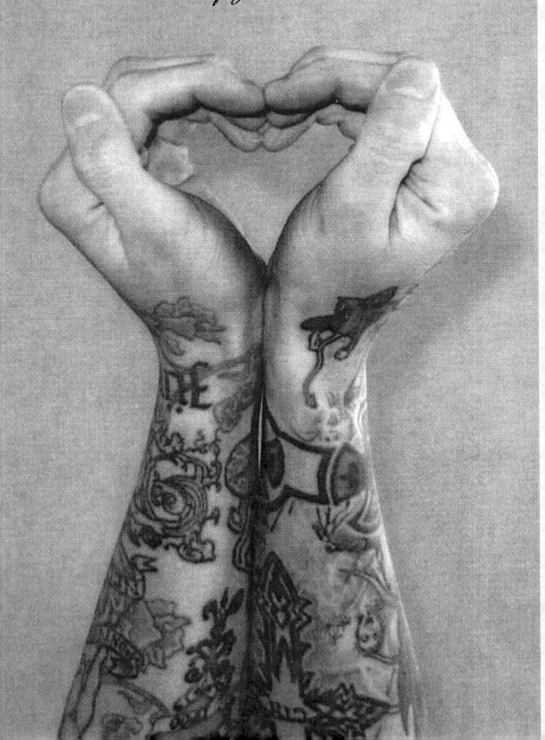

TOMORROW PROMISED TO BE FOREVER...
Photo by Yves Navant

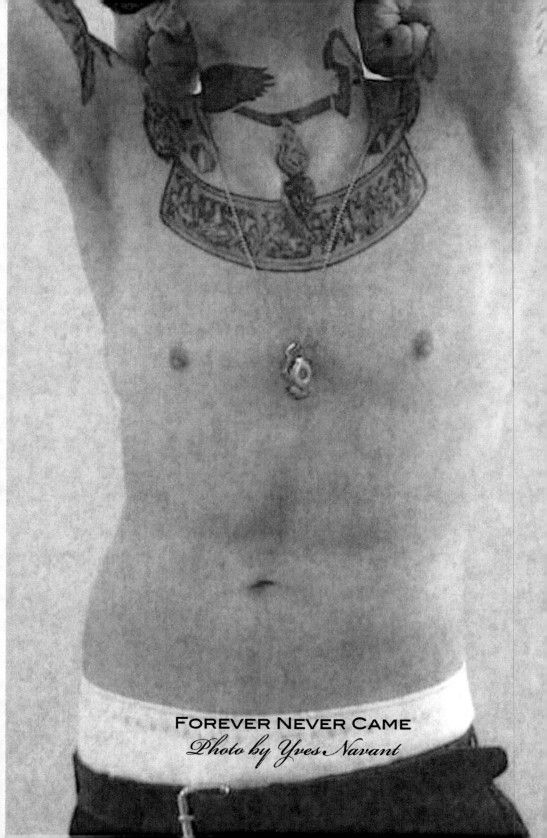

FOREVER NEVER CAME

Photo by Yves Navant

DEATHSTAR RISING
Photo by Agent Lain

MISCHLING
Photo by Florian Bailleul

INFINITE
Photo by Camille

A FUROR FOR THE FÜHRER
Photo by John Rose

WE LOVE ALL ENEMIES
Photo by Kent Sanchez

TH3 PORTRA1T OF DOR1AN GRAY
Photo by Daniyil Onufrishyn

Brand Recognition and the Cult of Personality 1.f

Photo by Johnny White and Yves Navant

WE HATE PHILISTINES
Photo by Daniyil Onufrishyn

Brand Recognition and the Cult of Personality 2.h

Photo by Johnny White and Yves Navant

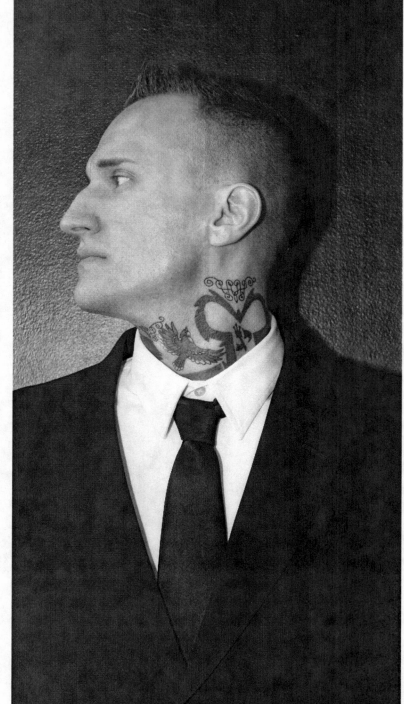

TOWARD TOMORROW
Photo by Daniyil Onufrishyn

Chapter 14: THE PERPETUAL SACRIFICE OF YOUNG SAINTS AND THE GRAVE FIFTH DEATH

I continued to write music with D' and run around the city like a self-made emperor; in reality I had next to nothing, but I stomped and danced and posed like the entire world was mine. I walked like a king and spoke like a general. It's funny. When you're in a speeding car, everything is whipping by you in a blur; you don't realize that you're about to crash.

There were so many ridiculous evenings; I was kicked out of the Church one Sunday night. I ran into a guy from high school named Chris Vigil in the bathroom, Jeremy and Wendy were waiting outside. Chris Vigil was cute in an ethnically nondescript way; I think he was on the baseball team in high school. Or basketball. Who cares? Chris and I talked and laughed and then returned to our respective friends. After I danced and had another drink, I returned to the men's room and Chris "happened" to be there. We stood next to each other at the urinals and I could tell he was looking down toward my cock, I smiled and said, "Come on."

Chris followed me into a stall and meekly looked up at me, asking, "What are you going to do?"

Just before the dirt kicked up and anything good happened, a security guard came and bounced us out of the club. I was pissed and stood on the trunk of Wendy's car, waiting for she and Jeremy to come outside. I saw Jeremy staggering up the block, sauntering with a cocky swagger. He saw me and shouted, "Fucking Kristian causing trouble! The Damage Twins are at it again!"

Jeremy and I had begun to sarcastically refer to ourselves as the Damage Twins, an appropriate appellation due to our shared fondness for drinks, trouble and destruction. I was Jeremy's white brother and he was my Native American kindred spirit. The Damage Twins. I shortened Jeremy's name to J', as I was usually in too much of a rush to speak more than a single syllable.

J' and I met a kid named Colby, he liked older guys and tattoos. I knew I had him in my pocket. Colby was only 19, so he couldn't club. Instead, J' drove Colby and I around the city in the rain while we listened to music and drank cocktails. Colby and I ended up in the backseat, sharing a drink while Jeremy drove. Jeremy chauffeured us around the city, winding the car through the oily, rain-streaked streets. Colby and I began to kiss; he tried his best to go down on me in the backseat of J's car; I stroked him off with one hand and held my big, huge vodka and orange juice in the other. Jeremy would periodically glance in the rear view mirror, our eyes would meet and I'd smile at him while Colby worked my dick down his throat, Jeremy would smile back at me and shake his head.

Jeremy's mom had come back to Denver to work as the Mayor's Director of Contracts and Finance. J' and I would pick her up at the end of the day from the Mayor's office. When she worked late, J' and I would wait inside, hanging out in a conference room, waving at the mayor of Denver as he passed by, walking from meeting to meeting.

J' and I met a young kid named Junior at Cheesman Park; we were bored and biding our time till nightfall. Junior told us he was 15 and complimented my tattoos.

Junior told us he was a hustler, a prostitute. Junior was working the park because he couldn't go home; his family didn't want a gay son. At 15, Junior was too young to work legally and so he was *working* the park. I wasn't sure if Junior was taking advantage of old men willing to pay for sex or vice versa; a mutually parasitic relationship.

Junior was cute in a disheveled, boy-next-door capacity; he spoke with a hoarse, tired voice. I felt an odd vibe from him, which was confirmed when he asked if J' and I were working the park as well; Jeremy laughed and dismissed him. Junior asked me to stay with him. I had been acquainted with a few prostitutes and I joked with Junior using the secret language and slang of the industry; we were talking about the prices being charged for various acts. I knew what the going rates were due to my familiarity with the trade. Junior assumed I was also a rent boy.

Junior's expression became serious and he flashed me a crucial look with his young eyes, "Damn. A guy like you?" he said, "I'd suck your dick for free."

I declined, offering some half-hearted excuse and I left. Those were my days with Jeremy and I loved them; it was all hustlers and bright sunshine.

On a cloudy Tuesday in April, 14 miles from my house, two teenage boys shot up their high school in a violent backlash to the bullying they'd received from their peers. I began to record the media coverage in real time. I felt sick as I watched the footage, a girl came out crying hysterically and reporters swarmed on her, she said, "He started bleeding all over and said that this was because people were mean to him last year."

I ended up using that quote as a sample in a song I wrote with D'.

The Columbine shootings had a profound effect on me; I could've been one of those boys, coming from the life I had, I could've been in their shoes. I survived the daily torture piled on me in my youth by sheer force of will. I watched in shock and awe as the day unfolded before me. I wish I could have saved them, I wish I could have rescued those two boys.

I empathized with those two young men. I wish I could go back and defend them from their asshole peers, save them from their daily abuse, save them from themselves. Tell me how you raised your kids and I'll tell you if they deserve to be shot. Did you teach your children tolerance and respect? Or do you allow them to cannibalize others? Do you look the other way when your children brutalize the meek and different?

BANG.

Wendy and I had plenty of adventure on our own, without J'.

At that time, the Snake Pit offered the most interesting and diverse crowd and thereby, the best time to be had. I met a Southern boy in the bathroom one night; I was always meeting guys in the bathroom. The Southern boy, with his slow verbal twang, seemed oppressively heterosexual. I don't remember his name. We'll call him John 1. John 1 was preppy casual in jeans, a polo shirt and a Ralph Lauren ball cap; he was attractively obsolete.

John 1 told me that he was a student at Denver University studying something I didn't care about. He said it was his first time at the Snake Pit. Obviously. John 1 stood next to me and unzipped my pants. We both stood there in silence till John 1 finally said those seven little words I loved to hear, "I've never done this with another guy."

The bathroom was empty except for John 1 and I; I pushed him into the stall beside the urinals and forcefully kissed him. John 1 and I drove our bodies into one another; we were kissing and grinding into each other. John 1 said, "I promise to make you cum…"

John 1 repeated that phrase over and over, growling in my ear and kissing and biting my neck, he kept saying, "I promise to make you cum…"

John 1 did his best to fellate me and then suddenly collapsed, he had some kind of overdose. I exited the bathroom as a club manager and policeman entered. I told Wendy we had to leave immediately. I took John 1's Ralph Lauren hat as a souvenir.

I was dancing on a podium a few weeks later at the Snake Pit, once the song ended; a nondescript looking young lad followed me into the bathroom. The lad looked like the typical college student; young, handsome and percolating stress just under his surface. We ended up making out; he'd always wanted to experiment with a guy. He asked if we could have a threesome with the Asian girl I was with. He meant D'. I explained that D' was a boy. The college kid, we'll call him John 2, went down on me with immediate ferocity. At the culmination of our tryst, John 2 dropped to the floor and removed a baggy from his pocket; he meticulously cut 5 short lines of cocaine on the rim of the toilet seat. Glamorous.

I talked a straight Mexican guy named Miguel into leaving his girlfriend at the club so he and I could stroke each other off in the dark backyard of his house. Miguel was a rivet head, his body was perfect and toned and hairless. We snuck through the fence of the house he rented, blocks away from the Snake Pit and exposed ourselves to each other in the moonlight. Afterward, he rushed back to his waiting girlfriend.

I briefly stopped talking to Jeremy after a night of out of control pleasure seeking. We planned a night out alone, without the safety net of Wendy or D's presence, even then J' and I were the most volatile of our clique. Together J' and I were dangerous thrill seekers on a take no prisoners mission for kicks, we'd have a good time or die trying. We went club hopping. The evening ended up with Jeremy stealing a beloved switchblade of mine for safety, he planned an adult rendezvous with a limousine chauffer we'd met that night. I didn't care if Jeremy was fucking a limo driver we met while clubbing. I was pissed that he took my knife. You can't just take a boy's knife. I refused to speak to him for months after that adventure.

Those nights were wild and amazing, entertaining and unrepentant.

And then I died again.

Tracks is a club in Denver that has always been dangerous for me; it's been an important location and is an integral plot point in this story. I made plans to hang out with Wendy on a Saturday night, we decided to go to Tracks, the biggest, most grand club in Denver; a multi leveled monument to music, alcohol, self-indulgence and promiscuity. At least that's what it was to *me*. The night began with Wendy and I enjoying a cocktail at my house before we headed downtown. We were perpetually on the guest list; expedience and preferential treatment were always nice.

Once inside, we continued to drink and found a table on the second floor in one of the massive, dimly lit lounge areas. This was Tracks' first location in Denver, surrounded by railroad tracks and nothing. Everything inside was glass and metal and flashing lights, a space inhabited by half clothed bodies, screaming for attention. I drank until the edges of all objects within my vision were slightly blurred. I drank till I didn't mind that all of the beautiful bodies and faces in the club were faceless. None of them really mattered anyway. They were all whores and imitators, I thought.

At one point I excused myself and headed for the men's room. After relieving myself I noticed the guy beside me; he was well-built and clean cut. Like every other guy in the club he was shirtless and perfectly built, except this guy had a long scar running down his chest, like rose colored candle wax had been dripped in a continuous line from the top of his sternum to his navel. Nothing is more perfect than imperfection. I wanted scars and damage and injury. I wanna know the person I'm with has suffered. I wanna see it.

As I dried my hands the scarred guy struck up a conversation with me and asked if I wanted to party. Of course I did.

The scarred boy and I stepped into one stall in a row of many and he immediately began kissing my neck. I felt his hot breath and I was instantly bored. I had danced this same dance too often with too many beautiful people. I felt nothing, neither high nor low. This was just another night, like so many before. My indifference was obvious to the scarred boy; he reached into a small pocket on the hip of his pants and with a troublesome grin said, "How about this?"

"Would this get you hard?" The scarred boy offered me a bag of white powder as though I were an alter and he were an eager sacrifice.

I knew if anything would start my engine it was that colorless dust. Speed was always my drug of choice. Dancing and fucking were always better on speed. The scarred boy and I took turns taking hits off the edge of a credit card he'd removed from his wallet. He opened my pants and knelt in front of me, leaving me to hold the bag and credit card. I took another hit. And then another. My head swam in the familiar feeling of white-hot acceleration. I could hear awful noises in the stall beside ours. I could hear muffled cries and mean grunts. It sounded like someone was working hard to hurt someone else, but muffled and wet, like the aggressor was covering their victim's mouth.

I had to see what was going on in the stall next to mine. With intoxicated, ambivalent eyes I saw a thin, twinky young man getting fucked bareback by a rough looking older guy, while another young man drove his dick down the twink's throat. I saw the little twink in the stall next to mine getting used and I felt nothing. Men drilled their dicks into the boy's throat and ass without mercy; tears welled in the boy's eyes. I

80

could tell the twink was in pain, but he liked it, moaning around the cock in his mouth.

My mind was spinning, my thoughts were moving so fast I couldn't catch them. I looked at the scene going on in the stall next door and felt coldly detached. I sank back down to the waiting mouth that continued to fellate me. I continued to inhale bump after bump of white dust from the bag he'd foolishly left in my hands.

I felt my heart pound like the fist of God was hammering in my chest and my mouth went dry. I could feel every single vein in my body. The veins leading to, and weaving up my neck throbbed and sharp pains stabbed my temples. I knew I was in trouble; I forced the scarred boy off my cock, pushing him down and away from me. I clumsily closed my pants with shaking hands and ran out of the bathroom, my now gray skin was covered in cold sweat. I was pulling posters and fliers off the walls as I passed. I was moving at super speed, I was moving so fast that I was an unstoppable blur. The world around me never stood a chance.

That overdose was the start of my fifth death.

Wendy delivered my remains, my corpse, to my home. I was an incoherent, trembling mess and quite miraculously, I managed to get inside. My hands were shaking so badly I could have vibrated myself through the locked front door. I could feel an anxiety attack building slowly in the lowest caverns of my chest, where my heart should've been. I was trying to will myself to sobriety, but my heart refused to stop pounding. My pulse was marching violently like an invading army on my wrists and neck.

I stumbled into the bathroom, my legs were wobbly and unsure, I lumbered like a baby deer learning to walk. I couldn't call anyone for help. I couldn't let anyone see me like this. I was functionally alone. I shook. I panicked. I collapsed in a heap on the cool tile floor, I was certain the floor of heaven was covered in cheap linoleum.

Everything I'd ever seen and done caught up to me at once, I had been wicked and I had done ugly things and my reckoning came like a gunshot. The mixture of guilt and drugs overwhelmed me and I was laid low, the emotional and psychological skin was ripped from my being.

Every emotion I had ever refused to feel, every mistake I refused to admit came at me all at once. Every heart I'd ever broken was now my own, every wound I'd ever inflicted on another now crippled my own body. My body convulsed and I choked on nothingness, it had been days since I last ingested solid food, I was vomiting guilt. I was riddled with emotional gunfire.

I suffered an immediate nervous breakdown.

I had died for the fifth time.

The aftermath of that death was excruciating; the following weeks were some of the worst I'd experience. I couldn't eat or sleep. I was drowning in guilt and regret and fear. I was afraid this death would prove lasting and would end my life with finality far sooner than I'd anticipated. I hated everything I had done in the name of fun. I hated that I fueled myself with drugs. I hated that I broke hearts. I hated that I had hurt people.

I was terrified that my kiss with HIV+ Larry, the night I trashed Hannah's apartment, would prove the kiss of death; I had bitten Larry and tasted his blood on my tongue. I felt Larry's disease flow into my mouth; I felt the red ribbons of death trickle across my lips as they wound around my mouth like a serpent. I was certain I'd killed myself.

My confidence and bravado was gone, lying in ruin on the bathroom floor. Now all I had was terror and remorse. For the first time I had fear.

If these words seem frantic, it is because that's how those days felt. Frantic. I don't mean to offend anyone. Please understand, my greatest fear was intimately tied to the one addiction I'll never be free of: sex. I acknowledge that I have a compulsive obsession with sex. I'm sorry if my relating of these events hurts anyone.

My emotional and psychological breakdown was so complete that the Kristian I had been truly ceased to exist. Any resurrection was in doubt. I had to know if I would live or die. I went to my families Doctor, a brilliantly selfless man named John Gale, for a battery of tests.

I explained my grave situation to Doctor Gale and described my hopeless and decimated mental state. Doctor Gale discussed the reality I was facing and comforted me as best he could. I had been seeing Doctor Gale since my childhood, I felt safe enough in his hands. Doctor's Gale's nurse drew blood from me and I stumbled out of his office into the warm July sun. I silently pleaded with God, I begged him for one more chance.

My nights were eternally sleepless; I laid in a silent panic, assuming the worst and preparing for my inevitable death. Finally, when I was too tired to go on, when I was completely exhausted, I would fall into a fitful, troubled sleep. On one such night, after long, countless hours of fear and desperate thoughts, I finally slipped into blessed unconsciousness. I couldn't sleep in my bedroom. I had to be in a room with a loud television, I needed the sound and flickering light to distract my racing thoughts. By the time I'd fallen asleep in the dark living room, the television had gone black and shut down.

I opened my tired eyes and the room was enveloped in a comforting blue glow, it was still late at night; or very early in the morning, depending on your preference. The TV, which had been turned off, was alive with luminous, living static and a figure appeared on the screen. The figure left the small, square confines of the television and flowed out toward me like an electronic wave. A beloved figure of iconic infamy and virginal renown appeared to me and spoke; I recognized her, she was beautiful and clean and radiant. She was wearing blue.

The beautifully immaculate woman stood before me and told me I would survive this trial. She caressed my forehead and told me everything would be fine. As she spoke I felt her light and life flow through me, I felt her energy caress me like a mother's love. The moment she was done speaking, my eyes rolled back and I returned to sleep, the first restful sleep I'd had in weeks.

I knew life had to go on. I didn't want life to continue as it had been; I wanted and needed to be a better man. Even if I were going to die, I had to be a better man. I decided I would no longer be the Kristian everyone knew, I couldn't. He was dead. With the exception of D', I hid out from any and all of my friends, refusing to speak to or acknowledge any of them. I promised D' I would return to writing music as soon as I healed. Music was art and I couldn't let art go. D', to his credit, waited patiently.

I told myself I'd never again go to a nightclub or bar. No more parties, no more strippers and drugs. Never again. Those things had ruined my life. Actually, allow me to rephrase that; *I* had ruined my life *with* those things. I own my mistakes; I understand and acknowledge them.

The phone rang just before midday, I answered and heard Doctor Gale's soothing, cherubic voice on the line. With calm lucidity Doctor Gale told me my test results were fine, I had no disease raging through my blood. I was negative. That moment began a series of regular and possibly obsessive tests to ensure my blood was clean. I needed the constant reminder to be good.

For the first time in weeks my heart beat once more.

I acquired a job at a local bookstore and soon began to thrive in the environment; I loved literature and the calm atmosphere inside the store. I loved the retired women leisurely thumbing through cookbooks; I loved the grandmother's browsing the shelves. At the time, that store was the drastic change of scenery I needed to recuperate.

During that era I refused to go out, I refused to step foot in a club. I became something of a recluse, afraid to let the wolf inside of me out, even for a second. I wouldn't speak to or associate with anyone except D'. I didn't drink. I never even considered taking drugs; I didn't crave them, I just stopped. Wendy and Jeremy were exorcised from my life. I had moved on and found fulfillment in a sedate and charming work-a-day life. I made new friends at the bookstore. I performed well and soon moved up through the company. So complete was my most recent resurrection that my new self was unrecognizable to the horrors and whores of the past.

I continued to write music and plan a fledgling career with D', this time without the nonstop partying. I insisted we change our working name to the New Gods, a signifier of my new lease on life. Under the New Gods name we began rehearsing for imminent shows and promoting ourselves. The New Gods were unique and talented ingénues, but we had much more to learn.

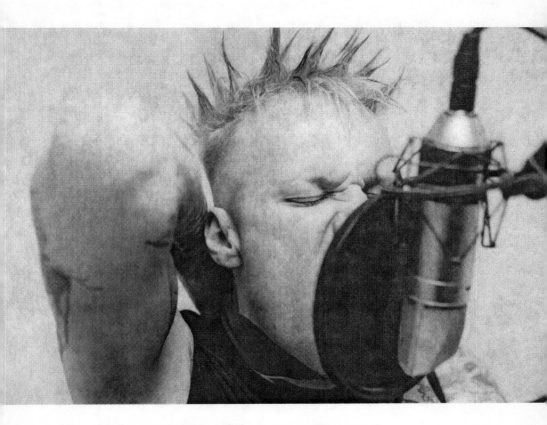

CRAWLING FROM THE WRECKAGE
Photo by Christopher Schadenfreude

There were moments when my past life tried to drag me back to hell; Jeremy and some unnamed henchmen vandalized my house in an attempt to force my hand against them, thereby drawing me out of hiding. I refused his invitation back to chaos. Wendy showed up on my doorstep unannounced, something that was and will always be forbidden, during a family party. Wendy was delivering gifts to my home in hopes of seeing me. I hid while my family made excuses regarding my total disappearance. As far as anyone knew, I'd vanished.

That summer renewed me, I finally felt alive again. I could try, I could pretend to be a normal young man.

Chapter 15: The World of the New Gods

My calm summer grew to a close with happy, contended shifts at the neighborhood bookstore and long studio sessions, where D' and I would write and often record at a feverish pace. D' and I modeled for publicity photos for the New Gods and I slowly realized I'd have to come out of my self imposed exile in order to make the band work. I was determined not to repeat the mistakes of the past and resolved myself to a new mentality. I could be around clubs and music and beautiful faces, but I could never degenerate into what I had been. I could enjoy a cocktail in moderation, but I set adamantine limits on what would be acceptable behavior for myself.

I didn't know it at the time, but I was wading back into familiar waters. If I had known what was on the horizon, I'd have clung to those brief moments of well-intended innocence. A leopard can never truly change his spots.

I knew I had to devote most, if not all of my time to the New Gods and I submitted a letter of resignation to the bookstore. D' and I were planning our first official show. We had been offered a Sunday night showcase at the Church, which I immediately accepted. The New Gods were to take the stage for two sets on a Sunday night in mid January. My life became an intensive schedule of rehearsal, promotion and preparation. I allowed Wendy to return to my life because she supported my creative efforts.

I posed naked, wearing only a respirator and black vinyl gloves for fliers promoting the show. The final photo was a full frontal nude; I stood emotionless in front of transparent drapery, while coldly assessing the camera and proudly displaying my genetics. I liked my body and I thought the over the top narcissism would be a fine way to keep people talking, anything in the name of art and reputation, and *anything* in the name of ascension.

The weekend of our debut, D' and I decided we needed more songs. We hastily wrote a cautionary tale called Chasing the Dragon and planned to perform two covers; Joan Jett's version of Do Ya Wanna Touch Me, which D' insisted was insultingly simple, and Judas Priest's Blood Red Skies. The original song, Chasing the Dragon, took an hour or two to compose from start to finish and upon completion, seemed like an adequate addition to our set. I left our rehearsal Friday evening repeating the melody and lyrics to myself over and over, trying my best to memorize the new song before our debut Sunday night.

Sunday evening arrived and I was primed and ready to explode; ready to walk on stage and own the night. The DJ played a set of heavy industrial intended to prepare the crowd for our show.

Showtime arrived, the house lights fell dark, D' had stolen samples from an obscure anime film and created intro music for us that typified the grandeur and theatrics we wanted to embody. A huge, booming voice echoed over the PA, "The New Gods have arrived!" I pressed my forehead against D's for a moment, to rally and psyche ourselves up. D' charged the stage and queued our sequencer to begin the first track, his guitar sounded my entrance. I strode onto the stage like a legendary general surveying a conquered battlefield. I growled "Hello Church!" into the microphone and spiraled into my alter ego of Kristian 13, a brutal and charismatic showman.

The first song, our original composition "American Tragedy" began and I swiped the sunglasses I wore off my face and violently threw them down to my feet. After the song ended, I dropped to my knees and felt an immediate shooting pain. The glasses had broken when they hit the ground and I had dropped my full weight onto the shattered lenses. Shards of plastic were stabbing into my knees, but I couldn't let the crowd know that. The show had to go on. The audience roared with applause, I got to my feet and the second song started. I clutched a strategically placed pair of scissors, hidden among our gear, and began cutting myself out of my clothes; before my vocals began I was left exposed in my skin tight, white under garments. The rest of our songs flowed perfectly, D' and I were a well-oiled, well-rehearsed machine, but only for those first songs.

Our first set ended and I was high on adrenalin and applause. A tiny part of me was relieved and excited that an audience of strangers had heard and enjoyed the music D' and I spent months writing. I approached the bar and asked for a shot of vodka, the bartender complied and I grabbed a paper napkin from the edge of the bar. I poured the vodka into the folded napkin and pulled the plastic shrapnel from my knee, cleaning the wound with the stringent alcohol. D' and I took a break to run around the club and socialize before our next set began. The crowd was filled with compliments and congratulations.

We took the stage once again feeling stupidly overconfident. During our first song, a handsome young man rushed the stage, he was screaming and applauding and trying to get on stage. The young man was quite obviously high, he pawed at me, grabbing my legs and yanking me down to my knees. Security pulled him away, I looked back at D' and we exchanged a satisfied look of accomplishment. The new song, Chasing the Dragon began as the security drug the young fan out of the club and I drew a blank. My mind had gone completely dark. No file was loading, no lyrics were appearing on the screen in my head. D' saw and recognized my predicament and continued playing. I adlibbed some hasty words and a melody, the audience applauded and shouted. The song ended after an eternity and the lights went dark, I looked to D' and simply said, "Fuck."

To our credit, D' and I quickly recovered. During one of the songs following the Dragon debacle, I materialized small cards featuring the band's logo and the nude photo I had posed for. I threw a stack of the cards into the crowd and one of the attending promoters looked shocked, he scrambled to the floor and tried to pick the cards up before any audience members had the chance. He couldn't stop them all and I loved it. I loved the chaos. I loved the alternating looks of titillated surprise and shock on the faces of those in the audience who picked up a card. At that moment I was a star and I was exposing my art (and myself) to an adoring crowd. Thankfully, the rest of our second and last set went perfectly and the crowd embraced us fully.

D' and I hung out till the Church closed, I was exhausted and couldn't wait to go home. I hadn't eaten anything of substance in days and I was ready to crash. I was tired, exhausted to my core.

D' was poised to review the live recording and video footage we had shot that night and refine our stage performance; he was all set to schedule our next slew of shows. I, on the other hand, was ready to do something else. I had grown up wanting to be in a band, write music, dress dramatically and play shows. After that first night at the Church, I had *done* that and I was ready to move on. My resistance to working on more music also gave me a much needed and cherished respite from the agony of Jolene's company. I gave D' some flimsy excuse and made sure I was unavailable for writing, recording, or anything else.

Chapter 16: THE DAMAGE TWINS AND THE UNEXPECTED DEATH

I drew quite a bit and read voraciously. January came to an end and I was lying on my couch one cold February night, reading comic books when my phone rang. I recognized Jeremy's number on the caller I.D. I hesitated for a moment before answering. Jeremy smiled through the phone, he spoke as though nothing negative had ever happened between us and I remembered why we were friends. Jeremy said he wanted to hang out and he was coming to pick me up. I was in my underwear.

I ran upstairs to my room and chose clothes to wear. It was a Monday night; I had no idea what the hell people did for fun on a Monday night. Jeremy's car pulled up in front of my house, I could hear the thump, thump, thump of loud bass from his car stereo. I ran out to meet him. We drove too fast toward the city and listened to music much too loud. Jeremy pulled into the parking lot of a bar called the Brig; I would soon find out that it was a gay strip club. We got a drink and I absorbed the… patina of the establishment. A drag queen playing pool sang along (off key) to the song playing overhead. Onstage, a toned up twink gyrated himself free of his short-shorts. Gay strippers have always seemed silly to me; not a lot of them can actually dance and the visual of a man, no matter how attractive he is, dancing to pop music while wearing sneakers or black loafers is hysterical.

Hysterical.

After the Brig gave us a nice buzz, Jeremy and I headed further downtown toward an infamous bar called the Triangle, notorious for its sex parties, hidden rooms and exhibitionism. The Triangle had a history of vice-squad raids, it seemed like the perfect place for an exploratory adventure.

That evening Jeremy and I began a long tradition of reinventing ourselves nightly, we'd become someone else every time we left the house. We'd create new names and lives appropriate for the moment. I had grown bored being just one man. That first time I was Alex, a two-time felon running from his inevitable third strike. Jeremy was Scott, my intrigued new best friend who had picked me up hitchhiking in Arizona, right after I had been released from prison. We had made our way to Colorado looking to start over or start trouble. The next night we'd be someone else.

I was elated that Jeremy and I could hang out and have cocktails without causing any real trouble or jeopardizing ourselves. Our reconciliation filled me with hope and optimism, I thought Jeremy and I had finally grown up enough to socialize responsibly.

Everything seemed perfect. I was so naïve.

THE DAMAGE TWINS
Photo by Alexander Nevermind

Jeremy and I made a habit of hanging out on Monday; it became our regular boy's night out. I loved the attention Jeremy and I received, we marched onto the dance floor and thrust our way to infamy, we'd dance on each other like slutty Girls-Gone-Wild and the crowd would watch in awe. We were big, mean fish in a smallish pond. Charlie's was a gay cowboy bar that hosted a rock night, we were dancing there one Monday when an obviously smitten young man tried to stop us as we were leaving the dance floor, he said, "I've never seen anything like that before. Are you two from the west coast?"

I just ignored him and kept walking. Jeremy put his hand on the boy's chest and pushed him out of the way. In a cool, dismissive manner Jeremy replied "Whatever."

We told ourselves we were stars; we were cold, aloof celebrity monsters and we loved every second. The staff at clubs began to recognize us and refer to us as the Damage Twins, our self-anointed moniker. We caused a lot of trouble, danced to the best music, never waited in line and never paid for our own drinks. Ever.

I was rehired at the bookstore I had worked for over the summer. I clutched for normalcy and found some in a safe, familiar environment. I knew I also had to return to the nighttime, neon danger zone of clubs and trouble. I began living like a superhero, complete with alter ego. I was a mild mannered bookstore clerk by day and a wild, amorous antihero by night. During the day I was Clark Bent; at night I was Über Man. I would start my day with vitamins and green tea and then go out, running around the city with my Damage Twin. Finally, I'd end the night around 3am. Those were thrilling times.

I carried a camera everywhere I went. I would often stop thugs, skaters and whatever rough trade Jeremy and I could find between clubs and ask to photograph them. I would cloud an otherwise straight man's mind till he agreed to expose himself to me, often convincing the young man to masturbate. More than once I was fellated by the amateur models for my camera's greedy eye. My photo shoots often ended in an alley, up against J's car, or in some stranger's dark, unattended garage or driveway.

By then, I had done everything except go to college. Introducing myself to the world of higher education seemed like a logical next step.

I applied to, and was accepted by the only private, highly accredited art college in Denver. Shortly after my acceptance I thought I should call the college to inquire about cost of tuition, I had no idea if I could actually afford to attend. A pleasant woman told me over the phone that the college was offering me a full ride scholarship. I was absolutely overwhelmed with excitement and couldn't wait to tell my mum, I finally had one small thing with which to make her proud. In the coming fall I would become a college student.

I still had the rest of the year, I had the entire summer to go wild and rule the night. I still had one last, long, riotous gasp.

An unassuming man in his early thirties propositioned me at the Compound between drinks. Jeremy and I made the Compound our home base, we'd start our nights there due to the heavy handed bartenders, the drinks so strong they tasted like gasoline and the leering eyes of the men inside. The man that approached me asked me to spank him, I didn't have to touch his genitalia or allow him to touch mine. He just wanted me to come to his house after the bars closed and spank him.

J' and I stopped by the guy's condo in uptown after last call and I beat him. I beat him with a paddle, with a hairbrush, with my hand. It was dark inside and the luxury home smelled like aggression and leather. It felt like I couldn't hit hard enough, I couldn't strike with enough force to make myself happy. When I got tired, I tagged Jeremy in. The guy whimpered in sick satisfaction, he obviously had domination and submission fetishes and I was the perfect type to help him act them out: tall, blonde and commanding. I took Jeremy's studded belt from him and used it to whip the guy. I was striking the guy so hard it seemed like sparks were ricocheting off his ass at the point of impact.

We left the guy sweating and erect on his bed, I knew he'd jack off the second we left. Once we got outside I realized with horror that Jeremy's belt was streaked with blood and several rows of studs were missing. I had been hitting the guy so hard studs shot loose and were flying across the room. We both laughed hysterically and threw the incriminating belt away in a public trashcan on the walk back to Jeremy's car. For weeks Jeremy complained about how I had ruined his damn belt.

The next day I went back to work in a shirt and tie and helped people find books from Oprah Winfrey's suggested reading list.

I was working away at the bookstore one night, gleefully helping customers and genuinely enjoying the evening. I ran up and down the sales floor, helping patrons when a sudden, shooting pain rocked the right side of my skull. I was no stranger to pain but this jolt was so intense I nearly fell to my knees. My right hand tingled, like it had fallen asleep. I squeezed my eyes shut, hoping the brief, sudden pain would disappear. It did. However, when I opened my eyes, bright, white holes obscured my vision. I felt my knees shake and I panicked, I rushed to the bathroom to regain my composure. I sat down in the largest stall and buckled over, my hands were shaking and I began to panic. I clenched my eyes shut and opened them once again; my vision was still compromised.

I staggered to the break room at the back of the store, there was a girl sitting at the table, eating her dinner. I fell into a chair across from her and she looked up at me. I wanted to tell her I was in trouble. I wanted to tell her I desperately needed help. I could think these things clearly, but my mouth wouldn't respond. The only noise I could command myself to make was a meek whimper, like a helpless baby. It was at that exact second that I realized how utterly fucked I was. I knew there was something terribly, disastrously wrong with me. I tried to speak again and no intelligible sound came out. Again, I whimpered like a baby. The stupid, useless girl looked at me and smiled, she said, "You look like you need some chocolate."

My thoughts raced, I thought I'd write the girl a note, telling her to get me help. My right arm was useless; I swung it to the table top like lifeless meat but couldn't make it obey my commands. My panic increased to stark terror. I knew I was damaging myself with every second that passed. I was dying in the break room of a large bookstore chain.

I banged on the table with my left hand. My eyes begged the girl to get help, but I could only make guttural, pained yelps. The girl smiled awkwardly, stood up, threw her plastic dishes away and left the room. I was overwhelmed by terror. I couldn't speak, couldn't write and was afraid to stand for fear my wobbly legs would give out beneath me. I collapsed on the table in horror and despair. I shut my eyes and begged for God to grant me control of my body. I prayed for the ability to scream,

I prayed to be able to shout for help. This whole ordeal happened in a matter of minutes. I had gone from functioning young man to stricken, crippled mess within a few short moments. Finally, a manager came to the back room and found me, she brought me water and I was able to raise my head to drink. When I opened my eyes, the bright lights of the break room overcame me. I was left with a splitting, brain-crushing headache. I sipped my paper cup of water and after a few agonizing minutes, I was finally able to speak. My voice was tiny and broken. I slurred my speech as though I'd been drinking heavily. I explained what had happened in simple, sluggish terms to the manager, she asked me if I wanted an ambulance. I declined, instead the manager told me to call someone to pick me up.

I was pale and shaken and felt severe pain in my head unlike anything I'd ever felt before, a dull throbbing pain throughout my skull. I could only reach one of my sisters; she and her husband came to take me home. I needed help to get inside the house. Once I walked through the front door, I collapsed onto the couch and covered my eyes from the blinding light.

I died again that night. I had suffered a tiny, little stroke that threatened to do irreparable harm to my mind and body; an unexpectedly cruel and vicious transient ischemic attack, a mini-stroke. I returned to work. Doctor Gale visited the bookstore. I explained my attack to him and he assessed my condition, once again saving me in an hour of need.

Jeremy acquired Nine Inch Nails tickets and called to invite me to the show. We were frequently given tickets through the Mayor's office. I was working but agreed to leave. I instructed J' to get the proper clothes from my house and then meet me at the bookstore. On a sweltering summer night, J' cranked up the heat in his car to full broil, while I styled my hair in front of the vents.

After the show we went to the Compound where I met a gorgeous drunk name Julian. Julian begged me to take him home; Jeremy would escort us. A cop pulled us over on the way to Julian's. I was in the back seat; once again Jeremy was chauffeuring me on an ill-advised date. Julian drunkenly pawed at me while the officer checked our IDs and then set us free, telling us to be careful. Julian continued to grope me once we arrived at his house, he told us he had been adopted as an abandoned baby by a

Hispanic family. Jeremy scribbled, "Julian is a fake Mexican" on every available surface. I made it home as the sun came up.

The next day I went back to work in a shirt and tie and helped people find books from Oprah Winfrey's suggested reading list.

The Damage Twins were notorious; at least with bartenders and security guards. I went back to Tracks for the first time since my fifth death; I could feel ghosts brush past me as I walked through the door. Flower was there with his fiancé. I introduced Flower to Jeremy, Jeremy scoffed and refused Flower's handshake, which enraged Flower, he quietly threatened Jeremy under his breath.

Flower was jealous, I had fun with Flower but he was no Jeremy. I knew the two were both possessive and willing to fight to prove who was or had been my better, closer friend.

Jeremy heard Flower's threat and looked down to make eye contact. Jeremy laughed at Flower and I knew the situation could easily escalate; the two boys were puffing up their chests and barking at one another. Flower was a big kid, with muscles and reach, but Jeremy was one the most viscous, deviously violent fellows I had ever known. Jeremy was a street-fighting savant; he had the spirit of an underage cross-dressing rent boy, he'd cut you. I decided to separate the two before their posturing got me kicked out of the club.

Heavy is the head that wears the crown.

I smiled at Flower and patted his arm, saying, "It was lovely seeing you, have fun tonight!"

With that, Jeremy and I walked off in search of another adventure.

The next day I went back to work in a shirt and tie and helped people find books from Oprah Winfrey's suggested reading list.

Going out with Jeremy meant we'd have a blast, always. However, Jeremy and I were volatile. If Jeremy and I ignited together against the city, the night was a delicate, unforgettable rollercoaster ride. If we turned on each other, which was a rare but occasional occurrence, the night was a high-speed car wreck and there would be no survivors.

We stopped by one of my boy's houses one night, intending to leave him a note. We came straight from a club, our ears echoed with the music we'd left behind. Jeremy broke into the boy's car and trashed the inside; once outside he ripped the license plates from the car. Jeremy was acting out and being destructive for the sake of chaos. I began to shout at Jeremy, asking him what the fuck he was doing. A gawking neighbor came outside and questioned Jeremy and I. We panicked and left. Jeremy and I drove off, punching and shouting at each other. We said all the things only best friends can say to one another, the acid coated barbs sure to dig in to your flesh, delivered by someone who knows all of your intimate secrets.

The following afternoon, we made up. Jeremy was the only friend I could attack mercilessly and we'd still be best friends and brothers the next day.

I went back to work in a shirt and tie and helped people find books from Oprah Winfrey's suggested reading list.

Richie Fine, a cute but diminutive *adult entertainer* was stripping at the Brig, Jeremy and I stopped in for a cocktail between clubs. Sometimes we liked to go and taunt the dancers, throwing ice or change at them. Richie came to our table and made small talk; he complimented my tattoos, just like every guy that approached me. Richie rubbed my shoulders and said, " I love your ink, man. I can't get any, just in case I need to rob a bank or something. They're too identifiable."

I guess getting fucked on camera was okay; splashing your face across countless screens all over the world, while some other guy drills into you, forcing your face into a pillow is cool, but having tattoos makes you too recognizable. Silly gay porn stars.

Jeremy was dating a drug dealer with a weave whose name escapes me; I hated him. I had to drive the two of them home one evening after partying a bit too hard. The dealer was singing along to a song as it played on the car stereo, I ejected the CD and crushed it in my hand. I asked the dealer if he liked the song that had come on the radio and he said yes. I replied, "I don't."

I turned the radio to white-noise static and turned the volume up full-blast.

The next day I went back to work in a shirt and tie and helped people find books from Oprah Winfrey's suggested reading list.

The end of summer approached and I knew a new life awaited, my life as a student at a private college. Education seemed like a foreign and alien world to me. The closer I came to the reality of life as a student, the more worried I became. I was wracked by fears of inadequacy and doubt, I was afraid that at 22 I was too old for college. I was afraid that I'd be the oldest person in the classroom, or on campus. I was afraid I'd fail, the last time I had been a student I had been unsuccessful to say the least. I often discussed my fears with my mum, she'd say, "Don't be silly."

With mum's reassurance, I'd steal myself and keep focus of my goals.

Best mum ever.

Freshman orientation arrived and I woke up early, my stomach was filled with vomiting butterflies. I drove to the far side of Denver, where the campus was located, but stopped a few blocks short of my destination. I called the Director of Admissions at the college from a gas station payphone and left her a voicemail; I told her school wasn't my thing. I told her I wasn't gonna attend college after all. I thanked her for the scholarship, but said, "No thanks."

The Director of Admissions spent a week teaming up with my mum against me. They said I was too good, too smart to waste my life, my mum told me she wanted me to try. Throughout the entire week the Director of Admissions called over and over, she and my mum tried every tactic from bullying to bribery. I refused all advice.

That weekend, I went out with Jeremy, just like countless nights before. I went out with Jeremy and we were the Damage Twins. It was the same exact night as every other, since we were 16. The same, exact night. Our evening ended when I was kicked out of Charlie's; a bouncer found me in the men's room getting serviced by an unnamed young cowboy.

I felt my spirit crash to the ground; I hated myself for falling into old habits. I hated myself for not learning my lesson. I had turned my back on a full-ride scholarship and potential future to get my dick sucked by some faceless nobody in a nightclub. I'd danced this dance before, months ago. I hate repeating myself. I thought I was most certainly doomed to failure and anonymity.

That night was the first time I electively died, I had to; it was the only way another, better model could be born and thrive.

The next day, after a speedy resurrection, I called the Director of Admissions at the college, this time begging for my scholarship back, I told her I'd do anything for another chance.

Chapter 17: THE ACADEMIC WORLD PART ONE:
THE RIGHT HAND PATH OF RESURRECTION AND THE AGE OF ENLIGHTENMENT

The morning of my first day of college was bright and sunny. I woke up nervous and excited, but the vomiting butterflies were gone, replaced by ambition and a desperate need to evolve. The campus consisted of three converted office buildings on the East side of Denver. I still wasn't sure if I'd receive the scholarship I'd turned down. I decided I'd still attend even if the college refused to award me the funding. I'd take out as many student loans as necessary. I didn't have to. After that first tense day, where I'm certain the college was testing me and assessing my sincerity, I was informed that I'd receive the scholarship after all.

I was relieved and excited. I was determined to prove myself; I was determined to earn the scholarship. My studio instructors recognized my ambition and work ethic and praised them. I soon realized I loved Art History and Liberal Studies, I found I could paint a picture with words as easily as I could with pencils, pigment and computers. The first weekend of college I decided to finish all of my homework in one sitting Friday night. Saturday's sun was rising in the early morning sky as I finished only the lengthy assigned reading for my Art History class. The living room where I worked was bathed in warm crimson, then rust. I had worked through the night. With a heavy internal sigh I thought to myself, "This is gonna be hard."

I acquired a job as the evening receptionist for the front desk in the design building; I could sit at work and finish my homework every night while I answered phones. My daily routine was to wake before dawn, drive across town to the campus, attend class till 6pm and then work at the front desk till the campus closed at 10. If I worked hard enough in the evening I'd have free time after the campus closed and on weekends to go out with J'. The Damage Twins would survive.

I was proving to be a voracious student, devouring any knowledge offered to my ravenous mind. But, I needed to vent the pressure of college life. The harder I worked the more I'd need to decompress. My accomplishments had to increase commensurate with the depravity and hedonism I experienced.

Jeremy and I were leaving a club late one night when an attractive Persian lad approached me; he began to cruise me. I was intrigued by the prospect of visiting the Middle East. The Persian was a handsome masculine scimitar; he roughly pushed me against Jeremy's car and kissed me. Our tongues darted around each other like eels playing hide and seek. His warm body pressed against mine, the cool autumn air grew warmer around us. Like a lost wolf, my hands wondered across the young scimitar's hard body, his skin was tarnished copper and so smooth. I undressed the Persian completely; I was fully clothed. The Persian struggled to get his hand down my pants and around my cock as it strained against my clothing. I smiled, reveling in the power I had over this now naked, vulnerable scimitar.

I pushed the handsome scimitar away and jumped into Jeremy's car, he'd been watching from inside the entire time, idling the engine. We pulled out of the parking lot as the Persian scimitar cursed me. I heard a loud thud, something had struck J's car.

The noise startled me, I looked toward Jeremy, "What the fuck was that?!"

"He threw his shoes at us." Jeremy replied with a straight face, staring forward. I laughed uncontrollably.

I loved school; I'd wake up before the sun rose every day, no matter how late I'd been out. I began to play the role of the narcissistic elitist. I worked images of myself into every possible project. I wanted to stay aloof in the new environment; I wanted to be untouchable. In one studio class I was assigned to find a tool that I'd never used to make art and create a composition. I went into the bathroom with a pad of Bristol board and a bottle of black ink. I opened my pants and dipped my penis in the ink, stamping the silhouette of my dick on page after page of art paper. It was a terrible mess and I stained the sink while trying to wash the ink off my cock. I was hoping another student would walk in while I was working.

I've always loved showing off.

Halloween came and I dressed as an apocalyptic, high fashion angel; I was an Alexander McQueen nightmare. I wore patent leather knee high boots, a mesh shirt, black-feathered wings and a vertical red slash of makeup across my face. Jeremy was a matching devil.

We ran from club to club, leaving a brilliantly crowded Snake Pit and arriving at the Compound around Midnight or so. The Compound was packed; costumed revelers filled every inch of the club. Jeremy and I had a nice buzz on and we headed straight for the bathroom, to check our makeup. A drunken bystander made the mistake of insulting us. Jeremy made an obscene gesture inches from the drunk's face. I grabbed Jeremy's forearm and ran his hand into the drunk's nose and mouth.

I assumed the altercation had ended, but the drunk followed us to the bar, he slapped the back of my head when I leaned toward the bartender to order a drink. I looked back with a scowl and told the bartender, "We're gonna kill that guy."

Jeremy and I smirked at each other, we spoke the same non-verbal language; the language of the Damage Twins. I pushed Jeremy toward the drunk; my best friend became a Molotov cocktail, a deadly projectile. Jeremy punched the drunk with enough force to send him reeling back into a crowd of horrified and riveted spectators. Jeremy and I were ejected from the bar; I was still enraged. I refused to leave. The building next door to the Compound was under construction; we pulled loose bricks from the half-demolished walls and waited for the drunk to leave the bar.

I said all the things that I knew would rile Jeremy up; I worked him into an unseeing frenzy. The drunk exited the bar and we attacked him. I repeatedly swung the brick into the drunk's back, his neck and his arms as he tried unsuccessfully to shield himself. Jeremy and I were a fiendish, bloodthirsty machine. We had four arms of fury and we brought them down on the drunk over and over. I dropped the brick and began to use my bare fists. My arms felt like I couldn't hit hard enough, they felt weightless and tingled.

The drunk scrambled toward the Compound like a wounded crab, scurrying close to the ground. Jeremy and I decided we'd wait and attack him once more, I couldn't calm down. After a few moments a security guard walked out of the bar and approached Jeremy and I. The guard informed us that the parking lot was under surveillance and the drunk had called the police. The guard warned us to leave while we still could.

We ran to Jeremy's car and sped off, the ride home was silent. I wasn't proud of what we did, Jeremy and I got into a lot of fights. It didn't make us tough. It didn't make us hardcore. It made us animals. Damage Twins indeed. I emailed my art history instructor and the overseer of my work-study position, telling them I wouldn't make it to school or work the next day. I told my instructor I wasn't fit to be around real people.

The end of my inaugural college semester approached. My Life Drawing instructor had been the courtroom sketch artist for the Oklahoma City bombing and Matthew Shepard trials; he knew I was fascinated with those cases. I performed so well in Life Drawing that the instructor gave me two of the drawings he had done in the courtroom.

I had always quietly raged about Matthew Shepard's death. I dreamt that I would go back in time and find Matthew, tied to the fence and rescue him. I dreamt that I would reach Matthew in time to save his life. I dreamt that I would arrive during Matthew's beating, just as Russell Henderson and Aaron McKinney began attacking the small young man. I dreamt that I would kill both attackers before they had the chance to kill Matthew; I dreamt I'd shoot both Russell Henderson and Aaron McKinney to death, sacrificing both failed, obsolete lives to the Gods of Societal Evolution and Enlightenment. I dreamt that I would see Russell Henderson and Aaron McKinney's heads explode like piñatas as I unloaded a righteous storm of bullets into them. Then I would save Matthew, I'd hold him in my arms and rescue him.

But, those were just dreams, instead I had courtroom sketches.

I received keys to the campus and alarm codes for the buildings, the college stayed open till midnight during final exams and I'd be responsible for securing the buildings after all the students left. I passed all of my courses, excelling in most. I had finally learned to be a student.

Once the semester ended, I was off for a luxurious four weeks. I slept in, went out and partied and read comic books. The holiday break was wonderful.

Christmas came like a freight train, much too fast. My mum bought me a full-length black fur coat with red satin lining. So deluxe. Jeremy and I partied as hard as young heroes party, running from club to club and had a genuinely brilliant time. Jeremy and I never dressed for the season; we wore what we wanted, weather be damned. Jeremy and I would peal off our coats and stash them in the car trunk, then shiver and freeze till we got to the club. Once we were in view of club staff and patrons, the Damage Twins attitude would take over and we'd act as though it were 90 degrees outside. We'd silently repeat the Damage Twin mantra, "You must be cool." Jeremy and I could not let anyone see us in discomfort and we certainly couldn't let anyone see us succumbing to something as pedestrian as temperature.

Then New Year's Eve arrived. Jeremy didn't have a car to drive that night, so I was the chauffeur. I picked him up and told myself I wouldn't be drinking. We went to the Compound and I had exactly one cocktail. I remember the night being fun; it just wasn't the typical drunken symphonic debacle we usually experienced. I drove Jeremy home and was speeding down the highway toward Golden when I decided to turn off the interstate. I thought a side street would be a much quieter and safer route back to my home. It *was* New Year's Eve after all.

I noticed a younger man driving beside me. Not too young, but younger in the context of him being a reasonably handsome adult man. The man and I made eye contact and then I sped past. The young man's headlights followed me as I left the city. I was wearing my fur; it was hard to drive while surrounded by its massive, black bulk. I turned into a gas station and stepped out of my car to remove the coat. The young man pulled in after me, stopping his car in the farthest parking space, in shadow.

The young man sat in his car for a second watching me, I dismissed him and removed my coat. I instinctively knew the guy wasn't a threat. I could smell his intentions, like the scent of alcohol, lust, and impending regret.

My movements became fluid mercury; I liked being watched. I couldn't let an audience, an audience of one in this case, leave without a show. I removed my coat, slid it in the back seat and opened my driver's side door, I intended to get back behind the wheel and drive home. The guy pulled his car next to mine and his window slid down; he looked like someone's collegiate older brother, the guy next door. The young man addressed me in a casual manner, as if we'd been friends for a while.

I responded nonchalantly.

The young man propositioned me, asking if he could suck my dick. He was wearing a wedding ring. Happy New Year, whoever-he-was-married-to, your husband was cruising me in a parking lot.

I was flattered; I smiled and replied, "No thanks."

The young man seemed obsessed; he began to offer me money. I continued to refuse; the young man countered my refusal by increasing the dollar amount he offered. I noticed his hands trembling

I began to consider the insanity of this. I was sober on New Year's Eve and I was being solicited in a parking lot. I had taken off a fur coat my mum bought me and someone's husband, or fiancé, or whatever was offering to pay me for oral sex.

The young man announced a figure that I couldn't refuse, it seemed like easy money to make and if this guy wanted to fulfill a fantasy with me, that was cool. I was an expert.

I got into his car and he drove to the edge of the parking lot. I was nervous, waiting for police cars to surround us. I shut everything off; I turned off any and all emotion and concentrated on the money. I was a mechanical man, this guy's dirty dream toy. I let him open my pants; the young man pulled my cock free and mouthed a quiet, breathy "Fuck."

The guy went down on me and was working hard to suck me off. I kept watching the light reflect off his wedding ring as his hands slid all over me. After I came, the guy dropped a fist full of crinkled bills onto my stomach and I closed my pants.

"Thanks man." the young man said as I climbed out of his car. I drove off. I watched in the rear view mirror to make sure he wasn't following me.

No one ever told me how exhilarating it would feel to be treated like a commodity. It's flattering to be seen as someone's fantasy, it's intoxicating to know you're worth buying.

Winter break ended, my second semester began. I met an Asian girl named Naomi; she was talented and beautiful. Naomi and I hated each other at first but gravitated toward one another, spending increasing amounts of time together.

Jeremy and I went out for Mardi Gras; we partied like Denver was New Orleans. I had no idea just how close to the end we were, I had no idea things would soon fall apart.

A few weeks later Jeremy and I went out again. I don't remember what the date was; it was supposed to be an unspectacular night of wildness like all the others. Jeremy and I headed downtown to drink and dance and flirt with strangers. Everything was fine till the drive home, flashing red and blue lights erupted from behind us as we exited the highway near Jeremy's house.

I knew we were fucked.

Officers pulled Jeremy out of the car and issued a sobriety test, he failed and was arrested.

I sat in the car, waiting for my turn. An officer approached my window and asked for my I.D. I replied to all his questions with "Yes, sir" and "No, sir".

The officer left me in the passenger seat to run my I.D. in his cruiser. He returned to me and asked me to step out of the vehicle. He shined a light in my eyes and asked me to follow as he moved the light from side to side. I saw Jeremy getting handcuffed and shoved into the back of a patrol car quite against his will. The officer who had been evaluating me raised his head above mine and shouted to his fellow cops, "This one's fine!"

"Yes sir." I replied. I looked to Jeremy in the back of the patrol car; he was enraged and mouthing silent threats toward me as I got behind the wheel of his car. I saw J' point an accusatory finger at me and I knew he was shouting expletives in my direction, I just couldn't hear them from behind the plate glass windows of the patrol car. I pulled away from the scene of Jeremy's arrest and drove his car back to his house. I decided against telling Jeremy's mother and family what had happened. It was after 2am and I had class in the morning. I left Jeremy's keys in the ignition and climbed into my own car. I sped home in hopes of getting at least a little sleep before the coming school day.

I kept working and attending classes. I was determined to finish the semester. It didn't take long for Jeremy to make plans with me. I drove to Jeremy's house and walked downstairs to his basement quarters. I found Jeremy in his bedroom chugging copious amounts of water; he was flushing the court-ordered Antabuse from his system, a drug designed to make the user sick if they drink alcohol, most often prescribed to alcoholics. Nothing was going to stop the Damage Twins from having a good time, not even and especially liver damage.

I kept up the cruel and demanding double life; I was a private college student by day and a wild, hedonistic, bohemian by night. I worked tirelessly in my classes and was placed on the honor role for my efforts. I was on the Dean's List for distinguished academic achievement every term of my academic career. It was worth it. It was worth all the stress and sleepless nights and rigorous studying. I finally felt like I was accomplishing something.

My freshman year of college came to a close and I had survived! Initially, I had been so intimidated, I had been so afraid of failure. I didn't just survive; I evolved. I was learning just how much I was capable of and I was pleased.

Chapter 18: DEATH!
(IF THIS GUILT BE MINE...)

Summer; the weather was warm and beautiful. I'm a child of the summer and I loved the climate. I loved summer's heat and intensity.

I entered my department specific Illustration classes during that first summer term at college. I decided I'd take as many classes a term as possible, bloating my schedule with 18 credits, more than the average full time college student. I'd use up my full ride scholarship before anyone decided to revoke it and I'd also complete my degree faster.

I began casually hanging out with D' and we rather tentatively worked on new music. The intense drive and passion that had fueled the New Gods era had vanished. D's slow moving musical composition couldn't keep pace with my creative output, so I focused on college. I still enjoyed making music; it just felt like a hobby at the time.

The end of June approached and with it my birthday. I had no time to think about the anniversary of my birth in the face of my studies. School took precedence.

Denver's gay pride parade was usually held on the same weekend as my birthday, the last weekend in June. I wasn't interested in innocent celebrations of identity and community. I wanted sex, drugs and the end of the world. I wanted riots, love and danger. Be careful what you wish for, I guess.

It became a tradition to attend the parade with Jeremy, collect phone numbers, celebrate and run around the city the final Sunday in

June. I had decided not to celebrate my birthday or attend the parade that summer; I had too much schoolwork to do.

Jeremy convinced me to attend the pride parade with him and then celebrate my birthday; we were terrible influences on one another. I planned to spend the night on a true and typical Damage Twins mission; I'd sign my name across well-toned chests, drink, flirt and destroy. Afterward, I'd return home, lay down for a couple of hours and then get up to shower and go to my 8 am, Monday morning class.

I had made a deal with Jeremy that I'd drive the car for our night out if he drove to the parade. That was my first mistake.

The parade was like every other I had attended, there were handsome faces that caught my eye and bodies that made me want to defile them. Jeremy and I began drinking at the rally following the parade. There were tents serving cocktails in the midday sun. We grew tired of the rally and separated, intending to reconvene for the evening's festivities.

I knew I'd be driving and unable to drink, as a compromise I took a handful of amphetamines and drove to D's. After we worked on music for a while, D' left the studio and returned with an opulent silver tray. The luxurious silver tray held a bottle of Absinthe, a dish of sugar cubes, two glasses and a vial of chilled water; all the proper, laborious and dramatic accoutrements with which to serve Absinthe, the devilish green fairy. We finished our first glass of the milky green devil and D' served another. I watched as the clear, glowing green liquid became cloudy and foreboding as it filtered through a dissolving sugar cube.

I left D's house and sped down the highway feeling the radiant green buzz of Absinthe moving through my body. I remember I was driving so fast the highway screamed beneath my tires. You know the sound, when you're driving with the windows down and you can hear the high-pitched whine of the highway submitting under your wheels. The sun was setting in the early evening sky and I could see the heat rising from the pavement like a ghost.

I arrived at Jeremy's house and let myself in. Jeremy wished me a happy birthday and gave me my present: five long, clean, sharp lines of cocaine cut to razor perfection on a bedside mirror. I dropped to my knees and inhaled the first line. A sharp burning sensation raced up my sinuses, I looked up at Jeremy, he turned to me and smiled, flashing me the wink that all drug users share; the wink of acknowledgment when you both know you're behaving like monsters. I lowered my head and inhaled another fat line; I could feel my heart start to accelerate. My mind was instantly stretched across the familiar infinite highway. Jeremy had served up nihilism on a plate and I greedily devoured her once again like a perfectly white, virgin sacrifice.

Jeremy had mixed a drink; we always drank before we went out. A pregame cocktail we called it. Jeremy handed me the huge vat of alcohol and I tipped the glass to my mouth. Jeremy pulled his shirt over his head and looked down toward me; he said, "Let's go."

I scoffed at him and inhaled the last length of powdered Armageddon. Jeremy and I ran from club to club, the Compound was chaos; far too crowded. We went to Onyx, a goth club were D' and Jolene and all the other faux vampires were flapping their wings. Flap. Flap.

J' and I returned to the Compound. In an attempt to sober up, I swallowed the last of the amphetamines I had brought with me; it failed to do the trick. The pills *did* succeed in reigniting the flames lit by the cocaine I'd inhaled. A guy whose name I can't remember and doesn't matter was trying desperately to make me take him home, he was dressed like a jock and acted overly masculine. Jeremy got behind the wheel of my car and we agreed to hang out at the guy's house till we sobered up. The jock couldn't successfully direct us to his house; we drove and drove in circles.

I growled in impatience. Jeremy became frustrated and I commanded him to stop driving, I told the jock to get out the car. We were pulled over in the middle of the city; I wanted the jock gone. He wasn't worth the effort.

I pointed toward the street ahead and Jeremy pulled away from the curb and raced off. I can't remember the drive. I can't remember if we talked or what I said. I remember arriving at Jeremy's and getting out of the car. I remember Jeremy grabbing the sides of my face and saying something to me, he looked scared. I remember getting into my car and speeding away. Then I was on the highway, a song came on my stereo, I don't remember what it reminded me of. I yanked the stereo's faceplate off and threw it from my window. I was driving well above the speed limit. I was angry with myself for staying out so late. I knew I had to be in class, I knew I'd feel terrible in the morning. I couldn't drive fast enough to get home.

I heard a loud bang and my car rocked violently from side to side. I wasn't sure what had happened. I kept going. I was determined to get home. I drove for a few miles then heard another loud bang. The car slowed drastically. I tried to speed up.

"Just make it home." I kept thinking.

Sparks shot out from under my car. "Just make it home." I thought and gripped the steering wheel tighter.

I remember losing control as I tried to will my car to stay operable. Through my clouded mind I knew I was headed toward destruction. I knew I was on the verge of disaster. I braced, trying my best to minimize the damage to myself. My car was careening down the highway, sparks flying from beneath; I was trying to wait for an exit, I was trying to guide the two-ton pile of wreckage to safety. I saw an off ramp ahead; it was *so* close. My car became more and more difficult to steer. The off ramp grew closer to me; it was just a few hundred feet away. I was so close.

Suddenly my car lurched and toppled. I rolled off the highway and down the embankment as though God was an angry child and I, inside my car, was the toy he had tossed aside. My body jerked from side to side, my face smashed into something hard, my nose collided with the steering wheel, my knees jammed into the dashboard. I could taste blood.

I remember thinking, "You deserve this."

I died.

I rapidly sobered to functioning lucidity as my car careened down the embankment, I tried to brace myself in my seat. I gnashed my teeth, waiting for the end of the brutal ride. The whole thing must have taken a few moments, but it felt like forever. My car eased to a stop at the bottom of the embankment and I assessed my condition. I had cuts across my shins and the bridge of my nose. I *felt* like I had rolled a car, but I thought I was otherwise okay. My car was right side up.

I could see a convenience store in the distance.

I told myself, "Just get home."

I drove my car toward the convenience store, sparks still shot from beneath it, but they were fewer and smaller. I thought I'd call my family for help. I thought I'd save myself. I made it to the parking lot of the convenience store and pulled myself from the car, like a fleshy bullet being rejected from its wounded mechanical body. I looked back at my vehicle and realized two tires had blown. I had been driving on bare rims, they began to cut themselves into strips, the shreds winding around the axle like wire, in the pale, yellow moonlight. I noticed the lights inside the store were very that I tried the front door and it refused to open. The store was closed.

I limped to an outdoor payphone and picked up the receiver, I wanted to call for help. I'd call collect. The world around me was abandoned. I was alone and broken in a completely foreign suburb of the city. I didn't recognize anything around me and there was no sign of life. I put the payphone's receiver to my ear and heard nothing. I angrily slammed the receiver down and then put it to my ear again. I realized the phone's chord had been severed. I was trapped. Stranded.

I got behind the wheel of my car, thinking I'd find another gas station, a grocery store, anything open at that hour where I could call for help. I was desperately looking for help.

My car became immobile; I was literally forcing it to crawl down the street. A loud grinding sound came from my bare rims hitting the street below. The night started out with the highway screaming beneath me in excitement, now the street groaned in pain and disapproval as my rims dug into its skin. I stopped in a church parking lot. Not a grand, luxurious church, this was the kind of church that exists in suburbia: a plain, beige box, surrounded by pine shrubs. I wanted to collapse. I wanted to fall on the cool green grass of the church and shut down. I left my car once more and struggled to remain on my feet. Through increasingly lidded eyes, I assessed the neighborhood around me. I saw nothing; no houses with lights inside, there were no living people anywhere near. I was crippled, trapped in an apocalyptic nightmare.

I knew I had made a disastrous mistake and I was ready to pay for it. I wanted to get home. I wanted to sleep in my own bed. I just wanted to get home. I wobbled toward a row of houses on unsteady legs. I just wanted to get home. I forced my body to climb the steps of the nearest house and knocked on the door, the porch was dark. I waited a few moments and knocked again; a light inside flashed on and then quickly went dark. I tried to speak to whoever was inside. My voice was meek and crushed at first.

"Please, help me…" I begged.

I received no response.

"I need help, I was in an accident! I need to call for help!" I begged the anonymous person inside to save me.

No one came and nothing happened. I resigned myself to abandonment and staggered back to my car.

I was cold and hurt, I was bleeding and I didn't know what to do. My eyes threatened to close and my body cautioned an impending collapse. I steadied myself against the battered frame of my car. I lowered my head in my hands and experienced an epiphany; no amount of wild, reckless fun was worth this. I continually pushed myself through various dangers, regardless of consequences, all in the sake of a good time. I should have learned my lesson long ago, but I hadn't. I just wanted to get home. I don't know how long I stood there, contemplating my own stupidity. Suddenly the night was on fire; the unassuming neighborhood was lit with strobing red and blue. The scene was alight with gaudy sirens; the police had been called. Finally, salvation would be mine!

I walked toward the flashing lights as they approached; as the lights grew nearer I realized there were two cars. I heard a voice boom from the vehicle, "Stop where you are!"

I knew I was going to be arrested and that was fine. I had broken the law. Probably due to my appearance, my copious tattoos and attire, the officers seemed to expect some kind of struggle from me. At the very least I think they expected angry, aggressive disrespect. They found neither. I may be a rabid and vicious rebel, but I feel compelled to behave respectfully unless extraordinarily provoked. That's simply how gentlemen behave. I thanked the police for coming and apologized for the situation. I referred to them all as "sir". I had to; I didn't know their names and that's what a gentleman does. I was prepared to accept the consequences of my actions. I knew I had to pay to play the dangerous game that my life had become.

The older officers seemed suspicious of my compliance and cooperation; they tried their best to instigate and annoy. I wasn't interested in reinforcing any outdated stereotypes. The younger officers appeared to understand my repentant, apologetic attitude.

One of the police cars left to survey the area, they wanted to make sure I hadn't killed anyone or caused any property damage. I assured them the only damage I'd caused was to my poor car and myself. I consented to a blood test to ascertain my blood alcohol level. I was handcuffed by one of the suspicious, older officers and watched as a tow truck picked up my wrecked and wheezing car. The corpse of my vehicle would be impounded and I'd pay a sizeable fee to claim its remains. At that moment I never wanted to drive again. The older officer tightened the handcuffs around my wrists enough to cut off feeling and circulation. I didn't mind; I'd been through worse. I shook my head at my negligent behavior and acknowledged that I would not make it to my 8am class as I'd originally intended. The second cruiser returned and affirmed that I'd not damaged or killed anything or anyone else. I told them so. The assembled policemen talked amongst themselves. A young, blond officer volunteered to escort me to a nearby hospital where my blood would be drawn. I thanked him as he approached. I was left alone with the young officer.

The young officer told me to turn around, he looked at my wrists and said, "Man, let me loosen these, your hands are turning blue."

I heard keys clatter against metal and the handcuffs slackened on my wrists, I could feel my fingers once more. The cuffs now rested low on each hand, just above my knuckles. I walked on my own and stood beside the backseat door of the young officer's police cruiser. I thought that's where bad guys went. The officer shook his head and opened the front, passenger door. The young cop was letting me ride shotgun. The sun was coming up. Happy birthday, Kristian.

We pulled into the parking lot of a hospital I'd never seen before; I didn't even know that area existed till that night. I still had no idea where I was. A nurse walked down the hall to meet us and led us to a private room where she drew my blood. I could tell the nurse and the officer were exchanging hand gestures above my head. I knew they were saying something to each other about me that I was not supposed to hear.

After my blood had been drawn the officer escorted me to a detox center where I was to spend the next handful of hours, I'd be confined till my blood alcohol content was below legal levels. I knew that meant I'd be there awhile. Once I had been processed at the detox center and all measures were taken to ensure a safe stay, the confiscation of my belt, boots and shoelaces, I toured the facility and once more shook my head. I was so stupid.

I had a little, tiny nervous breakdown and phoned my mum, she was less than excited to hear from me. The disappointment I heard in my mother's voice was worse than any punishment I'd receive. I kept telling her how sorry I was and eventually hung up the phone. One of my sisters lashed out at D' and Jeremy, unjustly blaming them for my mistake. My family was disappointed and angry with me. I deserved it. It was late afternoon by the time I was finally released. One of my elder sisters came to collect me and I collapsed into the passenger seat of her car. I was more thankful than I'd ever been to be going home. I was finally going home.

I regretted my actions and I was willing to accept whatever repercussions were necessary. I just didn't want to stop going to school. Whatever was going to happen to me, I just wanted to be able to stay in school. Nothing else mattered.

I researched the most frequently given punishments for driving while impaired by alcohol. I assumed the worst. I assumed my punishment would be the most severe. I prepared for my coming court date and began taking alcohol education classes, I had read that classes of this nature were very often assigned to people who commit alcohol and drug related offenses. I met with an attorney and she was surprised to hear that I wouldn't argue or fight a conviction. I knew I'd done something wrong and I had to be punished. The attorney told me I didn't need her help. Throughout all of this, I was still going to school and doing everything I could to redeem myself. I asked permission to leave early from my work-study position once a week in order to attend the alcohol education classes on the other side of town, near my house.

Golden had always been the place I returned to, to heal and recuperate, to make penance, to ask forgiveness. Golden was the womb I'd heal in and the cocoon allowing my chrysalis.

I was sorry to have become a cliché; I was a rebel without a cause who had stayed too long at the party. The judge at my assigned court date instructed me to complete the alcohol education classes I had begun and sentenced me to a lengthy probation. I'd also be responsible for paying court fees and costs. I was ordered to complete community service. I desperately wanted to deserve a second chance and I wanted something decent to come of my mistake. I met with a probation officer and she informed me of her expectations. After weeks of assuming the worst, after assuming I would be sent to jail, I had been granted a blessed return to life.

I continued my intense studies at school and worked feverishly to overcome my remorse. I let my probation wind down as I lived my day-to-day life as a student. I was tired of being a chemically fueled thug. I never wanted to risk so much of myself. I once again vowed never to see D' and Jeremy again, they were my enablers, they enjoyed seeing me explode and when I was with them I never stopped exploding. But remember, leopards will always be leopards.

My summer semester ended with serenity and hard work, with long hours spent studying and drawing. Without even knowing it, my teachers and classmates at school helped me recover from a well deserved, crippling sense of regret and guilt.

Chapter 19: THE ACADEMIC WORLD PART TWO: CHRYSALIS AND METAMORPHOSIS

I was nominated for a student ambassador position at school; an ambassador was an agent of the college, a peer counselor and tutor. Collectively, the student ambassadors were the closest thing the college had to a fraternity, or perhaps a sorority. I accepted the position in hopes of directing other young, creative minds away from the mistakes I'd made.

I insisted the Dean of Students hire Naomi, my new friend and classmate. I loved being around the energy Naomi projected; we grew closer and closer. Naomi came from a Christian family, the first time I met Naomi's mom she asked me two questions, if I respected my mother and if I believed in Jesus. Like myself, Naomi was a contradiction, she was spiritual and she adored her family but she was also boisterous, tough and opinionated. I wanted and needed Naomi around and I was respected enough that the Dean agreed to my request.

My fellow ambassadors and I were sent to a cabin in the mountains for an intensive weeklong training session. We were taught how to deal with peer crises and learned how best to represent the college. By the end of the retreat we were all best friends, and were all devoted to each other, our odd art school fraternity.

Our first official act was to help the incoming freshman class move into the dorms. I spent the night before move-in day in the back of a married man's SUV while he fellated me. I was video taping the encounter; I was watching someone's handsome husband worship me through the lens of my camera. The husband looked up at me with vulnerable eyes and asked me not to film his face.

The next morning I woke up at dawn and drove across town to the student housing, I was assisting the new freshmen as they loaded their lives into their dorms. Near the end of the day a black car sped into the parking lot, snowboards and a BMX bike were strapped to the roof of the car. The driver stepped from his vehicle and approached me. His handsome face was bruised in all the right places; he was a redhead. I loved redheads. The young man reeked of innocence and youthful charm; he had no idea how attractive he was, and he *was* damned attractive. He was the most beautiful, rough-edged thing I'd ever seen.

The world suddenly slowed to a breathless crawl, everything around me was a warm, throbbing neon blur. I could hear someone gasping for air, but the sound seemed far away, like it came from a tunnel. I realized after a few heartbeats that I was the one gasping. I heard music playing in the distance, it sounded like warm gold and reached a crescendo as the young man stretched his hand toward me with a mix of friendly curiosity and misplaced, awkward self-consciousness.

The young man introduced himself as Joshua. Damn him. I didn't want to be attracted to anyone at school, but I couldn't help myself. Joshua was inevitable.

Remembering my responsibilities, I escorted Joshua to the courtyard and introduced him to my fellow ambassadors and his new roommate. Throughout the rest of the day I noticed Joshua watching me as closely as I watched him. I wanted Joshua's stares to mean something. The night ended and we ambassadors wished our new freshmen class goodnight. My eyes clung to Joshua as I walked away, as his did to me.

Freshman orientation was scheduled for the following week; the first day was unspectacular. I woke up Tuesday morning; the news said a plane had accidently crashed into the World Trade Center in New York. One of the benefits of being raised by a paranoid, militaristic father is that you're always prepared for the worst. You expect catastrophe and invasion. I immediately and without hesitation knew our country was being attacked. I watched live as a second plane flew into the remaining tower. I hated being right.

The college had planned for the ambassadors to escort the new freshmen on a tour of Denver; we agreed not to cancel the event in the wake of national tragedy. The freshmen were a group of un-jaded 18 year olds, many away from their families for the first time. We were trying our best to distract them, make them feel safe and give them some semblance of normalcy.

I was a student ambassador and peer counselor trying to assure a group of 18 year olds that the world wasn't going to end. I searched the crowd for Joshua; he wasn't there. We boarded chartered buses and headed toward the heart of Denver. As we passed government buildings, we saw National Guardsmen in body armor standing on the rooftops with assault rifles.

I spoke up and tried to reassure the new students. I told them something like this attack was to be expected. I told the freshmen to think of the world as a public high school; every one wants to take down the privileged, popular kid. America was that privileged, popular kid.

The city began to shut down block by block, rendering our tour moot. The chartered buses arrived to drive us back to the campus; I was standing inside a furniture store with Naomi and a young Texan. We were watching live footage of ground zero on a huge television.

The Texan tried to choke back tears, through a thick southern drawl he said, "Why would anyone do this to us?"

"Because we have more than they do." I responded through thin lips and clenched teeth. We had more money, more influence, and a greater capacity to effect the world around us.

Balancing my second year of college took extreme effort. I spread myself between my classes, my work-study job and my position as an ambassador. I took all of my responsibilities deadly serious; I'd rather have died than neglect any one of them. I pushed myself to exhaustion and then found some small spark inside to force myself forward.

I was at work one evening when the phone rang, I answered with the customary college greeting. It was Jeremy. He had spent months worrying about me and missing me. Jeremy and I may have been an explosive mix but we were still best friends and he had spent months speculating about my condition and status. I missed him too, I missed the days of loud music and nights of wild abandon.

I knew my family would kill me if I went back to the life I had known and I would surely kill myself if I repeated my mistakes. Above all else I knew the mistake was *mine*, I never blamed anyone else for my accident. I did it. I drank too much. I took drugs. I wrecked my car. No one forced me to make those choices. No one put me in that position. I did all of that to myself. I would never allow myself to make that error again. I would protect me from myself.

I eventually agreed to go out with Jeremy, but the game would be different now. We'd use taxis to shuttle us into and out of the city. We'd use taxis to run us from club to club. I always requested a female cab driver. Taxis worked out beautifully for a while, till we got our confidence back. Once again, Jeremy and I were reunited in our shared love of mayhem and the pursuit of the non-existent perfect lover. The Damage Twins haunted the streets of Denver once more.

It was winter; I couldn't wait for the holiday break. I went out with Jeremy on a Wednesday night. I had been in class all day and worked till the college closed. After shutting down the buildings, I changed clothes and headed out. Jeremy and I were in rare form. Car crashes couldn't stop us. Death couldn't stop us. We ran from club to club, dancing and laughing. It was winter outside and the city was frozen; we lived in a huge, ornate snow globe.

We ended up at the Wave, a gay club on the edge of the city. The night wound down and Jeremy and I walked out with everyone else at last call. An ethnically non-descript guy clung to us as we walked toward Jeremy's car; he was short with an athletic build. The guy was okay looking and very drunk.

Jeremy was willing to drive once again; he was still on probation, as was I. I wasn't willing to take the risk of driving to clubs, Jeremy was. I let him. I was okay with Jeremy driving, he promised he'd be really, really careful. He swore.

We had parked the car a few blocks away, around the corner from the Wave. The ethnically non-descript guy struck up a conversation with us, he was trying to flirt with me. The guy talked us into getting into his car; Jeremy and I exchanged the look that we knew meant we'd cause a bit of trouble. The three of us got into the guy's car, a small, silver sports car. Jeremy was crushed in the backseat and I was the passenger. The guy asked Jeremy and I if we wanted to get high, Jeremy rolled his eyes at me in the rear view mirror. The guy began to grope me and I convinced him to undress. When he was completely nude I very discreetly picked up the guy's clothes, including his wallet and ID and dropped them outside the car. The guy was franticly fumbling with my pants; I laughed and said I had to run.

"Thanks for the rush, baby!" Jeremy snorted, as he climbed from the backseat like a spider.

I knelt down and snapped up the pile of clothes; I planned to hide them nearby. I thought it would be funny to make the naked drunk guy get out of his car and search the parking lot for his clothes and wallet. I was walking backward so the guy wouldn't see the clothes I was holding behind my back. Jeremy and I were about fifty feet away from the guy's car. The guy was still pleading with us to come back.

Suddenly two police cruisers pulled into the parking lot, the cars came to a screeching halt on either side of the little silver sports car. Two policemen ran to the guy's car and shined a flashlight in the window. The other two officers shined a light toward Jeremy and I. I panicked. I couldn't explain being drunk in a parking lot at 2am with some guy's clothes in my hands.

"You two stop where you are!" One of the cops growled at Jeremy and I.

Jeremy and I took a split second to look at each other in sheer panic; we were both still on probation. If Jeremy and I had been caught, we'd be in exponentially worse trouble.

"Put your hands over your head and get over here!" The cop commanded.

Instinct took over.

"Fuck that." I snapped and dropped the ethnically non-descript athlete's stupid clothes to the ground. This joke was over. I grabbed Jeremy's collar, spun around and dragged him with me as I ran in the opposite direction of the police and their accusatory flashlights. Jeremy and I disappeared in a cloud of fabulously evasive smoke. The two policemen and their angry flashlight chased us. I could hear the police stomping after us like horses. I took a second to consider what I was wearing, solid white from head to toe. White was awfully conspicuous, especially when one was trying to evade capture in the twilight hours.

Jeremy and I ran through an alley, the police were close behind. Jeremy spun his head from side to side, assessing the alley. Without missing a step Jeremy grabbed my shirt and pulled both of us to the ground. We slid under a wooden loading dock. We huddled toward the sparse shadows under the dilapidated wooden planks, hiding as best we could. Jeremy and I held our breath and watched as the cops ran past us. We waited till they exited the alley and then burst from hiding and ran in the opposite direction. Jeremy and I ran around a corner, we could see Jeremy's car just down the street.

My feet slipped out from under me. It was winter; everything in the city was covered in dirty ice. I was on my back, cursing Mother Nature. Jeremy looked down and smiled, he extended his hand to help me up, we couldn't keep from laughing. We rushed to his car. I looked over my shoulder just in time to see the two policemen, they had their backs to us and they had no idea we were just a few hundred yards away. Jeremy had leapt behind the wheel and started the car as I watched the two policemen.

"Get the fuck in!" Jeremy shouted and I complied. We sped off toward home and our continued freedom.

The next day I got up early, headed to college, went back to class and learned all I could.

I was beginning to realize I was destined to live a life of duality, balancing ambition with hedonism. Even if this leopard seemingly turned over a new leaf, no lamb had dare be fooled. I would always walk the line between good and evil. I wanted to be a hero, but when the nights were too long, in the dangerous hours before the dawn, I wanted to ignite and burn the world down around me.

I created a new identity for my non-existent band: Divine Reich. I thought it a clever play on a familiar phrase. Divine Reich would be the banner my work sat under, referring to a holy empire of intellect and societal betterment. I immediately used the name for a school assignment, a faux interview with a non-existent magazine. I planned to use the name for many pursuits: comic books, clothing, and an overall rebellious, revolutionary and anti-convention mentality. Divine Reich became my artistic brand and a social movement, even if I was the only member of the party.

An effortless four-minute drawing I did ended up in print, promoting the release of an upcoming movie I had nothing to do with. I was happy that I could consider myself published while still in school.

I began talking to D' again, he was my only outlet for musical creativity and thus, a valued asset.

I ran into Joshua in the college's gallery, his mother was standing at the front desk signing paperwork for a leave of absence. Joshua had broken himself attempting a death-defying trick while snowboarding. My handsome little daredevil. Joshua's shirt was cut to accommodate his injured arm and the plastic sling holding it against his body. More of Joshua's skin was exposed than I'd gotten used to. I could see his heartbeat at the pulse point on his neck. I could see the pale, lightly freckled skin normally hidden under clothing. I could see the toned, sinewy musculature of his upper arm and chest. I could see Joshua's pulse throb just under his jaw. I know Joshua was speaking to me, but for a moment all I could hear was his pulse. I could hear his warm heartbeat pounding in my ears like a drum. I could feel the blood rushing through his veins. I could smell him; his scent was radiating off of his skin like visible heat. Joshua smelled like a mixture of thrill seeker and boy-next-door, like shy adrenaline. My mouth went dry.

Without thinking I raised my right hand and placed it on Joshua's neck, we made eye contact and froze. Joshua had to know what my touch meant; I was betrayed by my hand's warmth and sincerity. Joshua and I stood unmoving for an eternity, each waiting for the other to react, my eyes pleaded with him to speak first. I surrendered. I told Joshua to call me if he needed anything. I walked away feeling like I had a fever. I knew I had to forget Joshua. I knew I had to get him out of my mind at all costs.

I decided to forget Joshua the same way I forgot anything I couldn't have. I'd call Jeremy and we'd take over the city for a night. I'd find a face that looked enough like Joshua's, or a body that felt like his when I touched it. I'd find a snowboarder or a BMX rider or some other fucking redhead. I would possess and devour Joshua's analogue as a sacrifice to my own frustration.

Naomi had gotten me extravagant Christmas gifts, including an opulent designer watch. I loved Naomi and her impeccable taste. I was going out with Jeremy on News Years Eve, logic and self-preservation dictated we take cabs to and from the city. D' had won a contest and was given a VIP section at Rock Island for the night; D' would be the king of a small, roped off area at a club I stopped going to when I was 15. Snooze. I certainly didn't want to go to Rock Island on New Years Eve, I mentioned it to Jeremy and we agreed we'd rather run around on our own than be forced to stay at that boring, old club. I neglected to mention my impending absence to D'.

Jeremy and I were picked up by a car service; a long, dark Cadillac drove us into the city.

Jeremy and I arrived at the Compound looking like reverse mirror images. I was dressed in white and grey and had spiky, platinum hair. Jeremy was dressed in black, his long, dark bangs hanging over his eyes. We ordered our first drink and climbed on top of a tall speaker to dance. The resident DJ noticed us and queued up a song that he knew would make us dance harder than anyone else in the club. We danced, receiving alternating looks of lust and disdain from the crowd below. Either reactions to our behavior satisfied Jeremy and I, we were up above the seething throngs, it didn't matter if they loved us or hated us.

We enjoyed another drink while the bartender called our Cadillac taxi to escort us to another club. The night was speeding up to a familiar and dangerous pace. I remember dancing on the speaker for one last, frantic song. I looked at my watch; the time was 10:Something.

I woke up the next day around Noon. I was lying on my bed, fully dressed. I looked at the walls closest to my head and saw what looked like dried streaks of bile crisscrossing in all directions. I heard my assembled family downstairs; they were all guests at my home, in the midst of their annual New Years Day celebration. My head throbbed. My chest heaved. I felt terrible.

By surveying my surroundings I surmised that I had died yet again. I didn't even remember this death.

I decided to undress and head downstairs for a shower. I peeled off the clothes I evidently wouldn't or couldn't get out of the night before. I was sitting in my underwear when I reached down to take my socks off. I felt hard, crisp lumps all around my ankles. With a cringe of fear I peeled the socks from my feet, crumpled up paper currency fell to the floor around my feet.

Somehow, I had gotten wads of money stuffed into my socks. I assumed that I had probably not stumbled across some very short, very charitable people; I knew the source of the money was most likely not good. I clenched my eyes shut, trying to recall how the hell I had gotten money stuffed into my socks but found no memory; the previous evening was covered by an impassable gray veil.

My fear grew when I realized the amount of money lying on the floor at my feet. I smoothed the bills out and counted them; there were hundreds and hundreds of dollars in the pile. Large bills. I put the money aside and walked downstairs, every sound my family made was magnified to an exponential degree. This was the wrong day to host a family gathering. I deserved the discomfort, I thought. I went about my shower. My mum commented to me as I made my way to the bathroom, "We didn't think you'd survive, we heard you choking and coughing all morning."

Evidently that was where the dried streaks of bile came from. I was aspirating in bed and had no recollection of it. I had been spitting up bile all over my walls, there was nothing else in my system to cough up. I bathed, I hung out with my mum and brothers and sisters, waiting for the end of the day so I could go back to sleep.

School was about to resume, I and the other ambassadors were preparing for the arrival of a comparatively small freshmen class.

Mysteriously I had not heard anything from Jeremy. Without him there would be no trouble before the new semester. I counted my blessings and went back to school. The difficulty and rigor of my classes was increasing. I was forced to take concurrent landscape painting classes, the introductory course and its follow up. I had to take them at the same time due to their place in the overall class rotation, waiting to take them in the appropriate sequence would negate my plan to graduate in an accelerated timeframe. I had long ago made up my mind that I would finish my Bachelor's Degree in less than three years; nothing would stop me from achieving this.

I hated painting. The classes were taught on location, in the middle of winter. I'd be standing in a rage at an otherwise lovely, but frozen park downtown, armed with a palette of toxic, messy oils, painting the surrounding flora and fauna.

I was home one night, working on homework when the phone rang. Jeremy had finally called me. I was excited to hear from him and asked him what was going on, Jeremy seemed surprised to hear such congeniality in my voice. I looked toward my stack of half finished homework as we spoke; Jeremy said he was trying to wait till I called him, but grew impatient. As our conversation progressed I could tell Jeremy was tiptoeing around something. Finally, Jeremy said, "Do you even remember New Year's Eve? Do you remember what you did?"

The second Jeremy uttered those 13 terrible little words, the gray fog lifted from my memory and I suddenly recalled New Years Eve's missing hours. I desperately tried to get the fog back; I wanted to forget. I reached for the fog in an attempt to cover myself, but it slipped from my fingers. Jeremy chuckled. I felt like vomiting.

I want to affirm that I don't advocate binge drinking or gorging oneself on drugs. I never intended to lose control like I did. In most cases, the intent was to go out, dance, pose for the onlookers and have a good time. Alcohol and drugs can be a slippery slope; you think you're having a great time till you realize you're sliding downward. Too many rebellious young minds have been destroyed by intoxicants. Too many rebels have burned out. I don't think any of this is funny. I don't think any of this made me cool or dangerous. I regret it.

While Jeremy chuckled, I remembered how he and I ordered one last shot at the Compound before leaving for The Wave; we were both in rare form. Jeremy and I mocked everyone else at the club and laughed at our own stupid, mean-spirited jokes. We stumbled onto the dance floor and thrashed about to the beat. Jeremy and I went together to the bathroom; he didn't trust me alone for fear I'd meet a handsome stranger and abandon him, I didn't trust him alone for fear he'd meet an irresistible pharmaceutical. Strength in numbers, it was the Damage Twin way.

The club was decorated for New Years, streamers and balloons were crammed in every available crevice, long strands of metallic beads hung from the ceiling. Jeremy and I tore it all down; anything in our path was crushed, broken or ripped from the walls and ceilings. We were so destructive. We were so stupid. After our trip to the bathroom, Jeremy and I went to the bar to order another drink. Then another. We were acting out, playing the stereotype of spoiled, nihilistic rockers.

Jeremy and I slid our empty glasses across the dance floor of the crowded club, watching as people stumbled over them. We threw empties to the floor, listening to the sweet sound of shattering glass.

It was cold enough that Jeremy and I had to wear coats, which was very rare. When it finally came time to leave, when we were on the verge of collapse, we sauntered up to the coat-check to retrieve our jackets. The coat-check girl was a vague acquaintance of ours; a jar in front of her was filled with twenty and fifty dollar bills. I snarled at the girl as she handed Jeremy and I our coats. Without breaking eye contact with the girl, I thrust my hand into her jar of money and clenched my fist. I withdrew an enormous handful of bills and barked at the girl, like I was clearing my throat. Jeremy's eyes grew wide in shock, humor and horror. I walked away, as though I had exercised my divine right, or more to the point, my Divine Reich. The girl leaned over the counter after me and shouted, "Hey! That's my money!"

Jeremy tossed a few bills from his own wallet in her jar and ran after me. I was strutting calmly toward the exit; Jeremy grabbed my arm and rushed me to the curb. It had just started to snow and the city was covered in glistening white. Jeremy gestured wildly for a passing cab; he was forcing me into the backseat before the cab had come to a complete stop. Jeremy ordered the driver off and the cab sped away as bouncers and security flooded onto the street from the Wave. The staff had been made aware of what I did and they came for me. Jeremy and I watched from the back window of the cab as security threw their arms up in frustration; we simultaneously broke into fits of laughter. In our mutually intoxicated state, Jeremy didn't notice me stuffing the money into my socks. I was hiding the money from Jeremy. I knew he'd ask for a cut, but he'd get nothing.

And that's how I accidently robbed a club on New Years Eve.

School was quickly becoming stressful and threatened to overwhelm me. Through no ones fault but my own, I was working myself too hard. I wanted to stay out of trouble, but had a penchant for poor choices; you begin to understand my chaotic mental state. I was determined to do it all, but maintaining my double life of academia and nighttime hedonism was killing me. I worked as hard as I could. Nothing mattered to me but my success. I was on edge every second of the day. I was sleep deprived. I was chronically exhausted and under weight.

Naomi and I had grown closer than ever, she became the best and most trusted of confidants. The line between very close friend and something more began to blur. A few weeks into the spring term Naomi gave me a cell phone, she'd maintain the service and pay the bill. In retrospect Naomi had given me a very expensive leash. I was flattered. I accepted the phone.

I had profiles online that included pictures and evocative but mysterious personal information. I never referred to my sexual preferences, I was always intentionally vague. Gentlemen didn't confirm nor deny their sexuality. I thought it was pedestrian. I got a lot of attention online; I got a lot of messages from men and women. Sometimes we'd talk and I'd give them my number.

I was on location in Denver with my painting class when my cell phone buzzed in my pocket. I didn't recognize the number so I ignored the call. The phone buzzed again, signaling a voice mail. The caller had left a cryptic message referring to a job he wanted me to do. The caller referred to how generous he was willing to be. I called the number back; the caller told me he was willing to pay me for a quick fuck. Based on my appearance alone, he assumed I was straight and wanted to pay me for sex.

The caller had no idea I'd performed for fiduciary compensation before. I let him hire me to play out his fantasy; I'd be a gay-for-pay heterosexual. He had, after all, offered me an obscene amount of money.

Also, I was very good at what he was asking for.

From the time I was a young man, I'd been with countless men and women. I'm not sure how many. I have a formula I use to acquire a close estimate; multiplying the number of people I'm with in a week and then multiplying that number by the weeks in a year, then finally multiplying that by the number of years since I became sexually active. The number is high. I'm not bragging. I'm not proud of my record; it's simple reality. If I could take them all back, I would. I'd trade all the countless, forgotten names for a handful of meaningful nights with the right person. But I can't erase my past. I can only live with it.

The caller told me he lived in a luxury high rise off Cheesman Park. The caller said he'd have me sneak in the building, past the security in the lobby; no one could know I was in the building. The caller told me where to park and how to bypass the guards and any other tenants. It was easy; his penthouse had a private elevator. The caller offered me a minimum of four hundred dollars to lure me over; my compensation would increase from that base figure depending on how far I'd go. And the caller wanted to go far, he wanted me to fuck him.

I agreed. I was going to be a rent boy one more time. I was gonna be an American Gigolo.

I tried to imagine my perfect lover as I drove. I imagined a beautiful and innocent looking redhead, toned and pale, with freckles on their shoulders, arms and back. I imagined undressing them on a pristine bed. I played that scene over and over in my head, on a perpetual loop. Being a gigolo wasn't new to me, I knew I was being paid to be the best. I was being paid to fulfill someone's fantasy. I wanted to do well. I wanted to live up to the caller's expectations. I wanted to be worth every cent. Ambition is king.

I parked my car around the corner from the caller's high-rise, a tall building stabbing the sky on the edge of the deceptively manicured Cheesman Park. It made sense that the caller's penthouse was on the edge of a park known for the dubious activities perpetrated there. From the street I walked into a parking garage and entered the private elevator. I could hear Giorgio Moroder playing softly in my head. After entering the necessary code, the private elevator rose to the pinnacle of the building. I had no idea what the caller looked like; I had no idea what I was walking into. I only knew the caller was a privileged asshole, willing to pay a well-tattooed young man for sex. Once again, my angular European face paved the way to adventure.

The elevator doors slid open like a mouth waiting to be kissed. I entered a penthouse that loomed over the city, tall windows revealed a panoramic view of Denver. The sound of running water was emanating from a bathroom at the end of a long, dimly lit hall. The penthouse was decorated with too many things; it looked like the owner or owners couldn't decide what they liked, so they bought everything. The floors were stone tile, the walls were covered with fine art, and everything was shiny. I heard the water shut off and the caller's voice reached out to me from the end of the hallway.

"Come in, " the voice said.

I walked through the penthouse, focusing on the task at hand. The gears in my head switched and I became Kristian 13, the man he was buying. I entered a warmly lit bedroom and was greeted by a very stylish and very well built gentleman in his forties; he had short-cropped dark hair and a perfect tan. The caller was wearing tight briefs. That's all. I had known men like this before; they were all the same, they wanted a diversion from their life, they wanted rough, anonymous sex. They wanted to pay for the things their partner wouldn't or couldn't give them. I cocked my head back in a cold, assessing gaze. I was literally looking down my nose at the caller. That's what he wanted; he wanted me to be tough. He was paying for the bad boy. The caller smiled at me and said, "Yeah."

The caller nodded toward a dresser against the wall, beside the bathroom door. I visually scanned the top of the dresser. I saw jewelry casually discarded, a Rolex, random rings, and bottles of cologne. Every photo in the room was facedown; the framed pictures were probably the caller's wife, girlfriend, husband, or boyfriend. Whatever. Whoever was in the pictures wouldn't get the chance to see me in their expensive, frivolous bedroom. I also saw a stack of bills. That's what the caller was gesturing toward; he was showing me a stack of bills. I understood; I spoke his language. I turned back to the caller with a smirk.

Ignition.

The caller approached me; he grabbed my arm and roughly felt its length, examining my tattoos. The caller turned around to show me his back; he had recently gotten a stylized sun tattooed between his shoulder blades. The caller was rambling on about how much it hurt. I put my hands on his shoulders and squeezed, the caller rolled his head back toward me. I ran my hands down his back, guiding him to the edge of his bed. The caller's knees were now inches away from the mattress. I gently placed my hand on the center of his back and roughly shoved him down to the bed. I quickly undressed and removed a condom from my pocket.

The gears in my head shifted again, like the engine of a high performance automobile. This was all second nature to me. I knew what the caller wanted and I gave it to him. I was the perfect, automatic lover. Buying my love was like driving too fast on a winding, mountain road; it was exhilarating and dangerous. There were times when the passenger would be a little afraid to lose control, but I'd keep them safe. In the end the ride was passionate and adrenaline-fueled and they'd have to return the car to the showroom. It was everything they wanted.

After I finished, the caller disappeared into the bathroom to clean up; I dressed and waited. The caller returned and retrieved the stack of bills from the dresser; he walked toward me and threw the money at my chest. I nodded in approval, splaying the bills between my fingers to ensure a satisfactory amount.

"Call me." I said as I left. I entered the private elevator and rode it to the subterranean parking garage, escaping the ever-scanning eyes of the lobby's security guard and cameras.

I returned to my painting class in time for the end of day critique. My classmates suddenly seemed fresh faced and doe-eyed. I knew I had just done something that most of them couldn't conceive as reality. I knew I was nothing like them; I was a different species. I swallowed hard and joined my classmates; I tried to forget what I had just done.

The Spring term was near completion; the weather was warmer. I was painting on location yet again. My phone buzzed in my pocket, I ignored it. Moments later, it buzzed again. I had a message. The caller wanted an encore.

I agreed to another session. I took a fraction of a second to consider how odd it was that a seemingly wealthy man was procuring my expertise behind the back of whoever was in those face down photos on his dresser. I told myself it was none of my business; I was product, available for the right price. The face in the photos and especially the caller's motivations didn't matter. I followed the same routine, stealthily gaining entrance to his building and using his private elevator to get to the penthouse. I found the caller naked, lying face down on his bed. As I stepped into the room the caller arched his back, raising his ass toward me. I peeled my shirt off and walked toward him.

After completing my work I discreetly removed the condom I had worn and stashed it in my pocket, with the wrapper. I never left evidence of my presence. The caller followed the same routine, this time he was more talkative as he walked into the bathroom to clean up. "You're fucking hot…"

I ignored the compliment and waited for him to throw money at me. I had already seen the stack of bills on the dresser; it was the first thing I looked for when I arrived. The caller smirked and crushed the bills in his hand before tossing them at my chest. I responded with a mean smile of my own and growled, "Thanks."

I returned to the park just in time to critique my painting with the rest of the class. I had pushed myself to evolve quickly; in 20 or 30 minutes I could finish an entire painting that was on par with the work of my classmates. I'm not bragging, merely giving plot exposition. It has to go somewhere. I'd rush through a painting and then sneak off to my car. I'd drive off to whatever adventure the day had in store and then return by the time class ended to present my finished painting and have it critiqued along with the rest.

He wasn't the only caller; my supplemental income came from men who needed someone like me, someone to give in to. I was an expensive, secret purchase and after working with me, those men could return to the dull, tiny person they thought they loved. Naomi soon took away the phone she bought me, after it became evident that I was never going to be her boyfriend. I liked to flirt, but I was nobody's boyfriend. I was glad to be rid of it; it meant all of those previous callers couldn't reach me any longer.

The frantic semester ended like a treacherous race. I was a wrecked car just past the finish line. I'd been working so intensely for so long that the sudden inactivity was a shock to my system. My idle mind began reviewing the previous five months; I'd evaded police, robbed a club and become a gigolo. A hero doesn't do those things. In the heat of the moment I hadn't had time to think about my actions, that blissful urgency was now gone. I was riding a wave of shock and revulsion at how easily I allowed my humanity to slip.

My conscience was like a plane going down in flames; I just knew everyone aboard was going to die.

Like an atomic reaction, my hedonistic behavior was self-perpetuating and ever escalating. I wanted desperately to be pure and divine and immaculate, but the baser things in life clawed at me like a sick, lustful ghost. There was an intensity and urgency burning deep inside of me, like a broken record that I couldn't lift off the fucking turntable. The fire inside me screamed out for love and romance and danger and violence. I had to feed the atomic flames or risk burning out completely.

I confessed to my mum. I had to, no one else in the world knew me like she did. I may have been a wild, rabid animal, but I was still a momma's boy. I was overwhelmed with guilt and regret. I was able to function, but just barely. The spring sun was too bright; I could hardly stand due to my body's lack of nourishment and sleep. The sun beat down on me and I felt weak and near lifeless. I was shaking terribly and had a hard time concentrating. Eventually I collapsed; I fell to the ground like a discarded marionette with severed strings.

It took an exhaustive amount of will power and the help of a therapist, but I eventually pasted my shattered spirit back together. I had no alternative; my senior year of college was approaching. I crossed my fingers, hoping my repairs would hold under the coming pressure.

I was raw steel and my life was a furnace. Every knife needs a stone to sharpen itself on. Every white-hot blade needs an anvil to be tempered against.

Chapter 20: THE ACADEMIC WORLD PART THREE: ASCENSION

Summer! This would be my final summer term at school, the last time I'd be enrolled during the bright, beautiful months when days are at their longest and best. My mind was naked and thus exposed, able to imagine wonderfully new things.

My classes were amazing, philosophy and psychology balanced out my rigorous studio courses. We Senior level ambassadors each proposed new students to be interviewed for recently opened positions; we each chose students who we felt could represent the college; students we thought could grow to be part of our group. We were a fraternity. We were family. We were a cult.

I went out once or twice with Jeremy. We were at the Compound, living the Damage Twins life. We saw an innocent and otherwise handsome twink and were filled with rage; the twink and I were wearing the same shirt. Jeremy and I thought that was unacceptable. I think Jeremy and I had seen him before, we were certain the twink had disrespected us on an earlier night. Who knows? Who cares? The twink was with two or three friends, stereotypical clichéd gays; worked out, primped and pretty. Jeremy and I followed the twink and his friends out of the bar at last call. Jeremy and I were soaked and looking for trouble, like always. We walked beside the twink, taunting and threatening him, "You better take that fucking shirt off."

The twink stared straight ahead and said, "I just wanna go home guys. Just leave me alone."

Jeremy and I *couldn't* leave him alone; the atomic furnace roiling between us had already been stoked to critical mass. The twink and his friends reached their vehicle, a small, black sports car parked along busy Broadway. I was afraid the twink would escape. The passenger side door opened, I shoved him hard against the doorframe, pulling my arm back to swing at the young man. How tough. How glamorous. I was menacing a defenseless kid for wearing my shirt, how bloody stupid of me, how juvenile.

Before my punch could connect, the twink disappeared in the tiny backseat of the car. I thought our altercation was over. Jeremy was never one to give up a hunt so easily; he leapt in the backseat beside the twink. I could only see Jeremy's long, insect legs dangling out of the car. I heard a blunt, wet "POP! POP! POP!"

I craned my head into the car and saw Jeremy pulling his fist away from the twink's face, he had struck the twink; three fast jabs to the nose and mouth. Instantly, a red waterfall flowed from the twink's nose; I could smell blood. Jeremy and I laughed, I grabbed his arm and we casually walked down Broadway, back to our car. Jeremy and I leisurely strolled down the twilight streets as though nothing happened; once we got into the car our misplaced and pointless rage flared up once again. There was an empty glass bottle on the floor at my feet. Jeremy sped past the little black sports car; I threw the bottle out the window, watching with loving satisfaction as it shattered against the driver's side door. The twink was in the backseat; a friend was assessing his broken face. The twink's friends all jumped into their car, the black sports car tore out of its parking space. The brave lads were chasing us.

A ridiculous high-speed chase followed, like you'd see on a primetime police drama. I loved it. I hung my head out the window, taunting the pursuing car. Jeremy sped the wrong way down one-way streets. The black sports car overtook us and swerved, stopping diagonally in our path. They thought they were cutting off our escape. What brave boys. Under different circumstances I'm sure I would have fallen in love with young men so willing to chase down their antagonists. Fate had cast us as enemies so I was resigned to play the role. I knew I'd be loving them with every strike, worshipping them with every punch. I assumed a street fight would ensue, I was ready, it wouldn't have been mine and Jeremy's first. My assumption was wrong. The driver got out of his car and dialed what I assumed to be the police on his cell phone. I would have been happy to fight my way out of a four-against-two battle; I was not excited about possible police intervention.

Jeremy jerked his steering wheel, spinning around in the street. We were facing the wrong direction again and more importantly, facing away from the black sports car. The tail end of Jeremy's car was scarce feet away from the twink's vehicle. I knew our escape was up to me. I growled and jumped from the passenger seat, as Jeremy gripped the steering wheel. I ran toward the guy holding the cell phone and struck him, backhanding the phone from his clutches. The phone clattered to the ground and disintegrated into pieces. I stomped on the wreckage, digging my heel in to ensure the phone's destruction. I ran back to Jeremy's car, hopped in and we raced off. We left the twink and his stunned friends in our wake as we sped to safety. Seconds after turning a corner and racing toward liberty, Jeremy and I turned to each other and began laughing hysterically.

Life wasn't all drunken brawls and forgotten kisses from strangers. For every night out with Jeremy, for every night filled with chaos and trouble, there were days and weeks filled with hard work; studying, drawing, painting, and design. I'd slave over a computer, trying to master the ever-expanding world of technology. I was still hungry to learn and hungry to prove that I was more than a vicious, wild thug. I knew I could only achieve evolution through education, work ethic and ambition. Every day I pushed myself to the limit and beyond, academically and mentally.

The new ambassadors were hired; one of them was named Jason. Jason was a fellow illustration student; everyone seemed to love him. Jason possessed some nebulous quality that everyone found attractive or disarming, he was smart and kind. Jason worked hard and wanted to be successful. We knew nothing about Jason's past or family. We took this wolf at face value, assuming he truly was a harmless little lamb. Everyone loved gentle, beautiful Jason.

I applied for and received highly competitive portfolio-based scholarships. I performed well as an ambassador and retained that scholarship as well. This was all on top of my initial full-ride; I would receive checks for thousands of dollars at the start of each term. My ambition bore fruit; I was being paid to attend college. I bought a white

Cadillac Deville; long and sleek, with red leather interior.

My college friends threw a birthday party in my honor, at an apartment overlooking the city. More guests than I'd invited attended, most brought gifts. My fellow ambassadors shut the lights off and walked into a crowded room with a candle-lit cake. I blew the candles out and wished for happiness and success. That party was remarkable, not due to any chaos or the booze we all ingested, not because of some pointless, soon to be forgotten sexual encounter. That party was unforgettable because we were all young heroes, the future stretched before us with unending possibilities. Youthful, brilliantly creative minds were there as guests in my honor. I wasn't a monster; I wasn't a space vampire. The world was ours, and once more I could try, I could pretend to be a good man with good friends.

Jeremy and I met up for the annual Pride parade on Sunday morning, the first since my accident. I was determined to remain in control; I wanted an innocent night of fun. After the parade Jeremy and I stopped by the Compound for one quick drink before heading to Jeremy's house, we'd bide our time till sundown. We pulled into the parking lot behind the Compound and I saw a beautiful, Teutonic blonde carrying trash to a dumpster behind the bar. I jokingly said to Jeremy, "There's my date for the night."

Jeremy and I went inside and ordered a drink; the blonde walked over and introduced himself to us. His name was Hans; he was a tough, masculine and pale Swede. Hans had the blondest hair, like strands of sunlight, his eyes were crystal blue. I decided he'd be mine. Jeremy and I talked to Hans for a few minutes before finishing our drinks and heading out. I told Hans we'd be back.

I kept my promise; the Compound was our final destination for the night. Jeremy and I arrived after midnight, walking past the line of hopeful guests outside like royalty. My eyes immediately found Hans; I walked through a crowd of statues on the dance floor toward him. We stepped in close to one another, he smelled like alcohol. I tried to imagine what he'd taste like, I was sure he'd taste sweet, like candy. We danced together; Hans pressed his body into mine, I clutched the back of his neck and squeezed tightly. We kissed under the strobing lights of the dance floor. After the song ended, Hans and I walked outside to get some air. Hans and

I devoured each other in an alley lit by neon, on a perfectly warm summer night. It was a cinematic ending to the evening.

I was on my way home from school the next afternoon when the Cadillac I bought broke down on the highway. Infuriated that the vehicle betrayed me, I abandoned it on an embankment. I accepted $75 from a tow company for the traitorous car.

I loved summer so much, the warm, sometimes-overwhelming heat, and daylight till 9pm in the evening. I met a man named Caine in a wealthy area of Denver. I don't think Caine did anything professionally; he lived a life of frivolity. Caine spent his afternoons at the gym, sculpting his football player build; he was a broad shouldered brute, and I liked it. The night I met Caine, at a bar in Cherry Creek, we discussed my tattoos; he said he wanted one. The next time I saw him, days later, Caine had gotten flames tattooed from his wrist to his shoulder. I'd drive to Caine's house after school, we'd hang out in his bedroom. We'd kiss. Caine would lift me off the ground when I tried to leave, refusing to set me down till I promised to stay a while longer.

Inevitably, final exams came. I was on campus 16 hours a day. I had planned elaborate projects for my finals, designing a line of action figures based on my family. I sculpted, painted and packaged the toys.

I planned a theatrical presentation for my Psychology of Creativity class; I planned to show the effects of positive versus negative reinforcement by praising the work of the majority of my classmates. I'd single out one student, a volunteer, and berate him till the point of emotional breakdown. The barbs exploded from my mouth toward the unsuspecting volunteer, I viciously attacked the lad till I saw his big, doe eyes fill with tears. Success! My objective was to educate my classmates on the power of language and intent; such small things as words can raise someone's spirit, or crush it irreparably. My presentation enraged a tiny Korean classmate; she stormed out of our classroom in an emotional huff after confronting me with her diminutive, accusatory finger. I applauded the girl's exit and announced to the class that her response reinforced my theory.

The next day the tiny Korean girl was approaching students with a petition, rallying people against me. She wanted me expelled from the school. I overheard her trying to convince one lad to sign her rather ill conceived petition. I couldn't have scripted a more perfect response for the young fellow, he said, "Are you kidding me? Kristian will kill me if I sign this!"

He was right. I would have killed anyone who signed that petition.

Summer ended. During the break between terms, we ambassadors were sent on our annual retreat, miles away from civilization. We were removed from society, sequestered in a luxurious cabin in the middle of nowhere. We all went through the psychological and emotional training necessary to forge us into a tight knit family, similar to cult programming.

I took a walk with Jason, stars lighted the woods around our cabin, there were no city lights to diffuse and dilute the night sky. The stars were on fire, so bright they burned our skin and close enough to reach up and touch. The night was blacker than black in comparison to the radiant stars. We stopped beside a lake and laid beside the calm water, we discussed the future in grand, nebulous terms.

The ambassadors returned to the city and continued preparations for the incoming freshmen class. My brother Jacques had fallen in love with a childhood friend of mine and they were married in September, just before my senior year of college began. I arrived at the student housing the morning after Jacques' wedding. The ambassadors and I were helping the new freshmen move into their student housing, once again. I could still taste champagne from the night before; the sunlight burned my too tired eyes. By the end of the day I was exhausted, more dead than alive. My body rested like a heap of brooms on the stairs inside the complex. The heavy, metal exterior door of the complex slammed closed, someone had arrived, I couldn't bring myself to care enough to turn and greet them. The mystery arrival approached me, my head rose to see perfectly passionate, tragically misplaced love standing over me.

It was Joshua. I had to clench my eyes shut; afraid his radiance would burn my eyes out. Joshua had the setting sun to his back; a perfect halo of light framed his beautifully rough face; he looked as though he had spent the entire summer in the sun, doing the foolish things daredevils do.

Joshua's voice extended toward me like an uncoiling vine, "Kristian!"

My beloved Joshua, my heart and adoration given form and life; I refused to admit how much I had missed him over the long summer. I thought about him everyday, I had his face, his smile, and his scent playing on a continual loop somewhere in my head. Though I was constantly busy and often with someone else, Joshua was always close to me, in a hidden and violet place deep in my heart. The sky faded to the background as I looked up at Joshua, his features came into clear focus. I saw his ice blue eyes, dancing with life. I felt Joshua's presence all around me; flowers bloomed and blossomed into life, filling the space between us with intoxicating nectar. Clouds ran from the sky in fear they'd ruin the moment. The sun was suddenly brighter and warmer. I felt hot, like I had a fever.

Or maybe I was just imagining the whole thing; maybe those things, those feelings didn't exist at all.

Joshua and I talked for a few minutes; I was trying to say so much without saying a word. I was trying to tell Joshua I loved him by feigning indifference. I was so happy to see him, but I was exhausted. I was truly falling asleep on my feet. I told Joshua to call me, we shook hands, allowing our palms to linger just a second too long and then I walked out.

I began spending more time with Joshua, we'd spend Saturday mornings test-driving sports cars. We'd play video games at night, in Joshua's room.

All right, Joshua would play video games. I'd watch him.

Heaven's Heat Wave ©
Beautiful, inevitable
Joshua

Photo by Ashley Phibes

Joshua and I attended a party together, the first of the new school year. College parties typically follow the same itinerary; young minds use alcohol as a social lubricant. The air between Joshua and I was smothering me. I was there, at that crowded party, with the only boy I loved, but I couldn't touch him. I couldn't tell Joshua how I felt. I refused to. The tension between us was a physical object, a wall of heat one moment, a tower of ice the next. I escaped the music, smoke and shouting voices by walking downstairs into the basement.

The hostess was an acquaintance and classmate of mine. Her boorish older brother was attempting to sober up in the otherwise deserted basement. I don't know how it began, but the brother and I engaged in oral sex. I knew he had never touched another man, I knew he was a stereotypical college student in some small town thousands of miles form where we were that second. I didn't care. The only thing that mattered was that this moderately attractive idiot wasn't Joshua. I told myself I needed that experiment to cleanse the palate in my heart of Joshua's aftertaste.

My head dropped backward as the young idiot fumbled with my cock, trying to fellate me on his sister's bed. I closed my eyes and saw Joshua in my mind. I pushed the lad away and stumbled upstairs. I felt sick. I told Joshua I wanted to leave; we were walking out of the house when I realized the brother was stumbling after us. Obsolete heterosexual guilt welled up in the hostess' brother and had overwhelmed him in the few minutes since I had abandoned him in the basement. I told Joshua to wait in the car; I didn't want him to know what I had done.

In the days that followed the brother suffered in panic, he let himself drown in guilt and paranoia. The brother confessed the lurid details of his sinful experiment to his family. At his family's request, I happily submitted to an AIDS test; the family was certain that every sexual deviant, no matter who or what they were, carried disease. They were small-town folk. My results were clean, I offered them as proof and reassurance for the family and considered the ill-advised debacle concluded. I certainly wanted to forget the idiot brother's rough, clumsy hands and alcohol flavored saliva.

The ambassadors and I were model students and genuine assets to the college, but behind closed doors our group was a dangerous and lustful menagerie. We began to organize private, invite-only parties. Those nights would begin as well intended fun, but they'd reliably degenerate into orgies of sexual experimentation. We were hungry young creatives and we devoured one another.

We planned a party; this time the dress code would be formal wear. That specific party changed everything. We got together, we took photos, and we drank. We danced and laughed. I knew I couldn't drive myself home; I asked the hostess for sanctuary till I sobered up. Beautiful, harmless Jason immediately made the same request.

I was in a darkened living room after an epic evening; most of the other guests had passed out or gone home. I closed my eyes, patiently waiting for sobriety to reclaim my mind. I felt a presence next to me on the cold floor; warm breath grazed my neck. Suddenly Jason was on me, forcing his mouth on mine, fumbling with the zipper of my pants. I had never before been so aggressively seduced. I tried to stop him, telling myself Jason was straight and simply drunk, but he was so warm and wanted it so badly I gave in to him.

That first night lead to a passionately ill-advised affair. Jason wanted to explore his newly discovered bisexuality, as long as it was our secret. We'd sneak out of class and lock ourselves in a conference room, worshipping one another before returning to class, innocently rejoining our peers.

Our affair came to a fevered boiling point one night when I was closing the campus. Jason lingered as I locked up and shut everything down. I locked the front doors and shut off all the lights. I walked through the building to make sure no one was left inside. I was joking with Jason about all the places in the college we could have sex, we ended up walking down a hall lined with administrative offices. I opened the door to the President's office and Jason threw himself at me, pushing me backward onto the President's desk.

Jason went down on me, deep throating my cock while I looked up toward the ceiling. I was being fellated in the office of the college President. Jason began to sweat as he worked my dick down his throat; I felt a warm drop of perspiration fall to my thigh from Jason's temple. I ejaculated in Jason's mouth and he spit my pearls in a wastebasket beside the President's desk. I straightened my clothes and we walked out.

As I locked the door behind us, Jason smiled and said, "Best. Ever."

We said goodnight and that was that. I had just been fellated in the President of my college's office, that night had the makings of an epic scandal.

Jason began to panic, our affair was too much for him; our friends discovered what was going on and Jason crumbled under their scrutiny. Our boss, the Dean of Students, joked openly when she found out about my affair with Jason, she said I was like ice cream, everyone wanted to try at least a little. Jason turned on me, telling our friends I was possessive and obsessive. I retaliated with an attack campaign; I hung posters of Jason throughout the campus with "LIAR" typed across his face. I hung underwear Jason had left at my house in a display case in a busy hallway. I stole a logo he had created from his computer and replaced the text with the word Obsessive; I made myself a t-shirt and wore it to school, proudly displaying the label he had maliciously given me.

Jason had suckered me, he had seduced me and ruined our friendship; he had to pay. We were young and passionate and felt everything to such an extreme degree, too extreme a degree. We both began to see the college's counselor in an attempt to quell our very public, reputation-endangering feud. I had one or two appointments; the therapist made a resonant observation, she said, "Kristian, you're such an intense young man. Worlds happen for you in moments. You live entire lifetimes in the seconds most people take a single breath."

I knew exactly what she meant. I had lived so many different lives in such short a time. I knew I had to slow things down, but I couldn't.

I can thank Jason for my first kiss with Joshua. The night Jason's Graduation Exhibition opened Joshua and I were on the darkened, deserted second floor of the design building above the gallery, in an empty classroom. We were just talking, hanging out away from the crowd and noise of the opening downstairs. The room was quiet and dim; Joshua was close enough to touch, too close. I was so nervous. I had been utterly fearless with love and sex till that moment, but being alone with Joshua made me tremble as though I were ill, like I had a fever. I stepped toward

146

Joshua, our eyes slowly closed as we moved toward one another. The world around us stopped. The second hand froze on the clock. I put my hand on the back of his neck. Joshua laid his hands on my chest; they felt like a straight boy's hands, rough and tentative. Our mouths met and I inhaled sharply, like someone had punched me, like I'd lost my breath.

I sucked the totality of Joshua in, taking his breath into my body. I loved it. I loved Joshua. That first kiss was the most important kiss I had ever given or received. With that first kiss, Joshua promised his eventual, complete surrender.

The kiss would be agonizingly brief; the President's wife suddenly barged into the room. Joshua and I lunged apart. I instinctively covered my mouth, like I was trying to keep some small part of Joshua from escaping. The President's wife told us we weren't supposed to be in the empty room; she reminded us that the opening was downstairs. Joshua and I returned to the reception in progress.

Jason's commencement ceremony would be the following Friday. I was working at the front desk; administration was busily preparing for the ceremony at an events center downtown, an appropriately lovely venue. There was a black cloud over the President's office, he had just found out that his father-in-law had died and would leave town immediately following graduation.

I received a call from the Dean of Students, she ordered me to stop my campaign against Jason; she said she was afraid for her job and my scholarship. The Dean said Jason demanded that I not attend the ceremony; he didn't want to be embarrassed in front of his family. The Dean said Jason had threatened to tell the President what we did in his office; I would most certainly be facing punitive action after receiving oral sex on the President's desk.

Scandal.

However, *no one* controlled me, least of all someone like Jason.

I hadn't planned to attend the ceremony till that phone call. Jason's threat forced my hand. Before the ceremony I had to deal with Jason's threat regarding the President. I was in control of my own destiny; I would never allow another to hold sway over my life. No one was going to intimidate me. I had to take that power away from Jason.

I marched into the President's office and asked if he had a moment to talk, he said no, he had just found out his father-in-law had died and was on his way to officiate the graduation ceremony. I sat down and began speaking anyway. I calmly told the President about my affair with Jason. The President didn't know who Jason was; he couldn't figure out to whom I was referring. I continued to talk, telling the President Jason and I had had sex on his desk. I braced myself for backlash and fallout. I was ready to be fired and expelled.

The President looked up at me and nodded, "Kristian," he said, "did you learn a lesson?"

"Yes sir…" I responded with uncertainty.

"Good! I don't feel any differently about you. Now get out there and get back to work!" The President smiled and patted my back as I walked out of his office; the same office Jason blew me in.

My fearless mentality paid off in that moment. I had taken Jason's ammunition away from him and came out on top. Just like when we slept together.

I sped to the graduation ceremony, arriving just as The Dean of Students was stewarding the last of the graduates into the main hall toward the stage. The Dean's eyes went wide when she saw me; she was terrified, she rushed toward me.

"You can't be here! I'll get fired and you'll lose your scholarship!" The Dean's eyes welled with tears, she was as fearful for me as she was for herself. The Dean's name was Jen; she looked just like Betty Page. Adorable, overprotective Jen; I loved her.

I took hold of Jen's shoulders and reassured her. I told Jen I had already spoken to The President and given him full disclosure. I told Jen I was bulletproof and she was fine.

I swung the heavy double doors open and strolled into the hall to find a seat; the ceremony had already begun. Jason scowled at me from the stage and then looked away.

I won.

The fall semester was done. I had come from a world devoid of hope, where a sucking black hole took the place of my future, now I was four months away from graduating college. The winter break began with stylish drama; I grew very close to a pixyish classmate named Monica, we'd often spend nights dancing at underground goth clubs till early morning.

I stumbled across an anniversary pressing of Bowie's Rise and Fall of Ziggy Stardust and quickly became addicted. I indentified with the theme of the album, an alien dropped into a world of rock hedonism. I was a Space Vampire trying to be a good man.

I met a barista who worked evenings at an upscale club called Asia. The young lady invited me to see her work that night. Asia was a sleek, futuristic nightclub with a stark Eastern aesthetic. Asia was a leftover set from Bladerunner, the clientele were spoiled, bored youth. I went to Asia with two friends, a pharmaceutical enthusiast nicknamed "the Doctor" and a sickeningly handsome skater named Isaac; we made our way through the red light of the club, walking on transparent floors, to be seated at a private table. Asia had a full kitchen offering sushi made to order. The boys ordered and ate. I refrained, of course. At the end of the night we were surprised to find our tab had been taken care of; we consumed hundreds of dollars in alcohol and sushi, all compliments of our new friend, the barista.

The second time we visited Asia we weren't so lucky. We drank top shelf cocktails and the boys ate sumptuous sushi with the same abandon as our last visit. We were wild. We walked through the club with attitude, owning the room. We did drugs in the bathroom, and flirted with everyone in sight. We broke glasses and scribbled graffiti on the walls beside our table. At last call the barista thanked us for stopping by and informed us of our unexpected tab, all several hundred dollars of it. Apparently the girl didn't quite approve of us carousing with other girls. The boys and I fled and would've gotten away if young Isaac hadn't given the barista his real name and phone number. He was the freshest and least trained of us, he didn't know any better. The barista called the young man and threatened to involve the authorities; we returned to Asia and begrudgingly paid our bill.

I was at home at the end of the year, December's frigid nights seemed to drag on forever and the eventual dawn seemed like a vague promise, not a guarantee. I was waiting for my final semester of college to begin, letting my mind run free and unfettered. I've never smoked cigarettes, instead I preferred to blow plumes of imagination and thought around my head in ghostly rings; I mentally exhaled dreams and plans, letting them billow through the winter air like gossamer mist.

The senior exhibition was the defining moment in an art student's academic career. Typically, illustration majors displayed three pieces of art, all the same size and some business cards. Yawn. I knew my own senior exhibition had to be remarkable; it had to be operatic and breathtaking. I was dreaming of all the ways I could accomplish this feat. I considered faking my own death at the opening; I considered all kinds of things.

I reclined on my coach, getting high on imagination, watching ultra-violent films, reveling in the contrast between the more viscerally brutal scenes and scenes of love and passion. The brand name I'd created a year earlier popped into my head: Divine Reich.

I thought of the beautiful hypothetic girl I probably should have been sleeping with while I was laying next to so many men. I thought of the future and downtown Tokyo. I thought of amputees and their intriguing prosthetics. I thought of Jean Paul Gautier and Vivienne Westwood. I thought of amputees and high fashion. I thought of prosthetics and expensive jewelry. I thought of glamorizing severed limbs. People covet expensive rings and bracelets; I thought people should buy high-end, platinum prosthetics from Tiffany's, high fashion, pneumatic, designer pistons that would replace human limbs. A robot arm stamped with the Louis Vuitton logo in place of passé flesh and bone.

I thought of neon. I thought of tragic love and sex and downtown Tokyo. Again.

I recalled my intent to use Divine Reich as an umbrella, covering all of my artistic pursuits. I decided to write, illustrate and print a comic book for my senior exhibition. The comic would be called Divine Reich and include all of the ideas I had birthed while staring through the television as violence and love played across the screen.

The story synopsis was simple; an amputee with robot arms lived in a congested future city, he would save a beautiful girl from enslavement at the hands of an awful villain who just happened to look like my last lover.

I also planned to design, sculpt, and package a corresponding action figure line to display with my art. The toys, in addition to three huge, oversized pages from the interior of the book would comprise my senior exhibition. With business cards and my portfolio underneath, of course. I'd also have numbered copies of the comic on a podium in the gallery. Executing my plan promised to be laborious and I'd have to start work immediately, but it would be brilliant. Far above what any previous illustration student had ever presented.

I wanted it to be good. I wanted to impress people. I wanted it to be wonderful. I wanted to purge all of the negativity from my system. I wanted to be true to my imagination and myself. I wanted to make my mum proud. I wanted to make all my mistakes worthwhile. I just wanted it to be good.

I planned out the visuals and wrote an angst-ridden and nihilistic narrative for the book that very night.

Monica's beautiful sister Andrea visited for a weekend, I fell in love with her at first sight. Andrea was stark white, like a blonde lily; her curves were played by a classical musician and given form by God. Andrea was dangerously beautiful, she looked like she'd eat your love and you'd be happy to feed her more and more, till there was nothing left of you. Monica invited me to go clubbing with she and Andrea.

Joshua and I hung out Saturday morning, we drove to a car dealership near my home and test-drove sports cars. We raced up Golden's winding mountain roads. Joshua would kick out the rear wheels of the car on turns, swerving dangerously close to the edge; he loved any vehicle capable of great speed. Maybe that's why he liked me; *I* was a vehicle capable of great speed. I had my hand on the emergency brake; Joshua reached down nonchalantly and touched my hand. It was the first time we'd made physical contact in the light of day, I felt awkward and nude. I was a nocturnal monster, discovered in the too bright sun.

I rendezvoused with the girls that night, at Monica's apartment. I loved Monica and her glittering energy, but there was something different about Andrea. I could feel lust rising from Andrea's skin; she was radiant and seductive.

A group of us went out to a fetish club called Onyx, a goth-rock, fetish window into the mind of the Marquis DeSade. At that point, Onyx was the most hedonistic and overtly sexual club in the city. Dancers would twirl flaming batons onstage, wearing very little black vinyl. Onyx was a private playground where anything could happen; amorous young people could experience the pleasures of the flesh and experiment with taboo and secret desires. Couples would perform sex acts for the amusement of other revelers; every moment of a night at Onyx pushed the envelope of taste and socially acceptable behavior. It was Sodom and Gomorrah, and we loved it.

Soon after we arrived at Onyx that first night I climbed atop a podium and danced to something fast and angry. I was dancing for Andrea, dancing to seduce her. I was performing a modern dance of the seven veils for Andrea's viewing pleasure. When the song ended, I climbed down to reconvene with our group and an innocent looking skater, a true heterosexual remarked, "That was pretty sexy for a guy."

ANDREA,
MY
24 HOUR
JULIET
Photo by
Alexander
Nevermind

Onyx' official photographer spent ages pursuing Monica and Andrea; photographing them, capturing small parts of their soul in that soulless environment. I stole a few moments to lay my hands on Andrea; I put my arms around her and kissed her soft, perfect lips. Andrea and I fell in love, had an intense affair and broke each others heart's in the span of a single night. I was Romeo in a future wasteland, Andrea was Juliet, she left town and the curtain came down on our love story.

After that first night Onyx became a favorite nightspot. My friends and I would work ourselves to death at school all week, and then dress to kill, dancing our asses off at Onyx. We'd assign a theme to each night. I was very, very into the 1970's Glam scene and reinterpreted Bowie's Ziggy Stardust as a meaner, rough trade saint; a hustler from space, ever the space vampire. An acquaintance from my teen club days had recently been released from prison; he had been accused of killing a man. The lad had "Skin Head" tattooed across his shoulders and he was pretty damn handsome. The Skin Head and I danced together on a podium; we kissed aggressively, angrily pawing at one another for the club's viewing pleasure. I was wearing a leather collar; it smelled like the Skin Head for months. Onyx was a once-a-week carnival of sin, spectacle and lust. I fit right in.

The police raided Onyx, the media got wind of the depravity and fetish night was no more. Seems you can't have group sex onstage after all.

I met a wrestler from a state college online; his name was Wesley. We exchanged messages one night while I was working on art for Divine Reich. Wes had a thick, masculine body, short wavy hair and adorable blue eyes. Our relationship was built on a foundation of sex, nothing more. Wes was into Water Sports, he wanted the warm, wet love of other men to flow all over his tight, stumpy body. Wes met me on campus one afternoon, after I had closed the buildings. We had sex in the library, on a couch. Wesley was on his back fellating me; I was on my knees, leaning over his face. Wes begged me to get him wet, he begged for my warm salty love. I gave it to him and then we had sex on the floor. And then we had sex in the bathroom. I thought we were all alone, but there had to be someone locked in the building with us. The story of me fucking a big, built wrestler in various locations on campus became an urban legend. I surmised that another student had hidden somewhere in the building in hopes of staying to finish their work. I'm sure whoever that student was saw some amazing, amazing things that day.

In March Denver and the surrounding suburbs were crippled by a huge blizzard. The second the roads were slightly passable I drove to the campus to work on Divine Reich; everything was still closed, including the college, but I had to finish the project. I forced my car to crawl down treacherous highways toward the campus; I had to get work done, no matter the risk. When the roads were finally cleared I drove to Monica's, I hadn't seen any friends in days. As I was racing up a busy highway, I saw dark figures moving toward me at a fantastic speed. I continued to accelerate, rushing in the direction of whatever was heading toward me.

I could see four large horses coming into focus, stomping toward me, running toward incoming traffic. The animals looked fierce and majestic as they stampeded into the headlights of oncoming cars. You could see every rippling muscle on the animals as they bathed in a cocktail of silver moonlight and the artificial headlights; you could see every snort hang in a frozen cloud above their snouts. I evaded the furious equine quartet and passed a wrecked truck and trailer. The vehicle carrying the horses had been hit and the trailer's living cargo was now going wild on the highway.

I was spending every waking moment on my senior exhibition. I would close the school at 10pm and lock myself in, working till 4 or 5 in the morning. I'd race home, shower and return for classes. I took 30-minute naps in the library. I slept only when absolutely necessary and in the smallest possible increments of time. Divine Reich was coming together.

I foolishly accepted an outside freelance illustration job on top of my senior exhibition work. I was digitally coloring a comic-style pamphlet for some credit company. I was working with a writer who had written Flash for DC Comics. I would color panels of the pamphlet between printing pages for Divine Reich. The job added a tiny bit of stress to my already taxed schedule, but it paid very well.

I finished the Divine Reich comic, my toy line and all necessary work required to graduate. I was impressed with myself. I had finally accomplished something. I had finally done some small thing to validate my intelligence, work ethic and ambition. I had finally proven that I could survive and persevere. I was once a rebel without a goal. I had grown up living life night-to-night, never certain where I'd be the next morning or whom I'd have slept with. I had survived childhood bullying, my own dumb-ass choices and self-destructive behavior. I had been through so much in my comparatively young life.

I was scheduled to graduate with Magna Cum Laude honors from a private college. I had been on the Dean's List for Distinguished Achievement every semester and earned numerous scholarships. I would never have to pay a student loan. I successfully completed an entire Bachelors of Fine Art degree in two years and eight months. The college psychiatrist was right; lifetimes *did* happen for me in the span it took someone else to breath.

My senior exhibition opened on Friday, April 6th. The show was a huge success and I was the only graduate asked to sign autographs during the reception.

Naomi came to congratulate me. Jeremy and his mom came; they brought me an Indian artifact as a gift, a symbol of luck and prosperity. I loved it. My family threw me a huge party to celebrate. Afterward, Monica and I went out with a few other friends. I allowed Jeremy to mix with my college friends for the first time. Jacques, his wife and a childhood friend of theirs came along. My compartmentalized worlds collided. The night was wonderful; I worked hard and finally felt as though I made my mum proud. I had finally accomplished one little thing that I thought would make my mum smile. Everything was perfect.

Joshua called me the next day. I was sleep deprived from the long night out, Josh's voice dripped over me like honey. I told him I loved him. Joshua said I was the first person to say that to him.

The following week I graduated college with honors. Early in the morning, before the graduation ceremony, I drove to the Cabrini Shrine, a renowned and beautiful place of worship, high in the mountains overlooking Golden and the world. I think often about faith and spirituality; my maternal grandfather, a minister who I adored, lived for his faith. I've studied every world belief; I can indentify with several facets of each, I find certain resonant aspects in all of them.

Do I believe in God? I believe in a higher power, I believe there's something above us.

But most of all I believe in myself.

That's enough for me.

I stood in the wind on a mountaintop, beside statues and images of Jesus, Mother Cabrini and the Virgin Mary. I prayed for the future. I thanked God for allowing me to survive this long. I thanked Heaven for the chance to become something more than I was. I thanked my father for giving me charisma and charm. I apologized to every lover I had ever dismissed, every heart I had ever broken. I apologized for taking even the shortest seconds of life for granted. I said goodbye to every wasted day I had spent spinning my wheels and looked toward the sun, I looked toward the future.

I drove back to the city, to the graduation ceremony and once again, everything was perfect.

On Friday, April 13th I became a college graduate, with honors. April 13th. The same day my father had died.

Chapter 21: DEATHSTAR RISING

After graduating, I took a month off to sleep and regain my senses before starting a position as the evening receptionaut for the college. Receptionist doesn't quite do me justice; yes, I was a receptionaut. I loved the school and believed in what they did; giving young, creative minds direction and purpose. I believed in giving creative youth an education. The campus was also inspiring and absolutely insane with drama, so that helped. It was the perfect plan, I'd take over the front desk for the evening shift, the same job I'd held as a work-study. I'd be able to draw, build a portfolio and work on freelance material while still being paid to hold a "day job", even if my day job was at night. I never had to be at work before 1pm and got off at 10pm, I could still enjoy a full nightlife.

I spent months drawing and writing stories no one would ever read or see. I had a few brilliant ideas and a few less so. I would create and finish complete projects and then discard them. I saved some for a while; they were all eventually burned or shredded. I was practicing. I was bored. I began to slowly flesh out an idea for a Divine Reich story; I wanted to explain how the protagonist, a handsome amputee, lost his arms. I leisurely took my time drawing the pages for a book I wasn't certain I'd ever finish.

I modeled for a brilliant painter named Irene McCray. Irene was an elemental woman of astounding experience and technique; she interviewed me about my dreams, hopes and overall desires before ever putting brush to canvas. Irene was able to glean a keen understanding of my true character. Irene translated the language of my heart to the world and displayed my inner most spirit on huge canvases in vivid detail. I opened up to Irene as I would a psychiatrist and she understood me. At one point Irene and I discussed auras. She said mine was black; not because I was evil or sinister, but because my aura consisted of every color firing all at once, glowing so vividly it appeared totally saturated, it was black.

Irene was the only artist for whom I posed nude. I had already undressed emotionally and spiritually for her, my clothes didn't really matter.

Joshua's birthday was in October; he was turning 21. I took him out with a few friends for his birthday. It was a Sunday night and we went club hopping, we both had cocktails and danced. It was the first time I saw Joshua dance; he was just a little bit awkward, like a straight boy. Adorable. I was driving him home at the end of the night and we began to talk about our relationship. Our heretofore-unseen candor was probably due to the alcohol.

I told Joshua I needed to get him out of my system; my feelings for him were exhausting. Joshua wasn't willing to be involved in a gay relationship and I didn't really want to be in love. I parked my car outside his apartment and we continued to talk. I wanted to be over Joshua. I wanted to get past my feelings for him. That would be the last night I allowed myself to love him.

I turned toward Joshua; he was so perfect. His square jaw and handsome face was lit to perfection by the streetlights outside. We tried to make love in the front seat of my car. We were in a vehicle with fogged windows, surrounded by the steam created by our gasping mouths. The only noise was the sound of our racing hearts. We were working our bodies hard enough to collapse; I sweat Joshua out of my heart.

I helped my predecessors in the Student Ambassador program host a Halloween party on the college's campus. I entertained, spitting fire and creating a piñata for the guests. I had filled the piñata with cow hearts, lungs, tongues and other discarded body parts. I capped off the carrion cocktail with a soup of blood, Karo syrup and red food coloring. I wanted a damp, awful surprise for the underclassmen. I hung the piñata between two tall trees outside, in the dark autumn night. Students swung a bat at the piñata, diving into the shadows after it crashed to the ground and finally broke. The underclassmen reached into the darkness where the piñata had fallen in hopes of finding candy and prizes. They found none. One girl dressed as a blue fairy reached in and said, "Its wet!"

The blue fairy stepped into the light, she seemed ill, realizing she was covered in blood and red syrup up to her elbows. The front of her taffeta dress was soaked with sticky, sweet blood. Good times.

I collected redheads. I met another who lived in an apartment in Denver, around 9th and Downing, a gay sprawl of urban decay and not-quite achieved glamour. This one was well built, masculine and handsome. The redhead told me he couldn't host; he had a boyfriend. I met him outside his apartment building and we walked around his neighborhood, ending up in an alley where I fucked him. I returned once more for a second visit, that second time he let me into his apartment. He was watching Moulin Rouge and rambled on about the gay subtext of the movie, I didn't care. I didn't listen. Later, I stumbled across the redhead online, he was doing porn under the pseudonym Blu Kennedy.

I went out with Jeremy for New Years Eve, we ushered in the New Year with a flurry of drugs and alcohol. I remember choking a girl with her Hermes scarf as we danced. The night ended with a typical Damage Twins disaster, Jeremy lost his wallet somewhere between fistfights, drunkenly stumbled dances and kisses with strangers. We called for a cab and the driver drove me back to Golden and then escorted Jeremy back across town free of charge. Such a nice guy.

I woke up the next day to a house full of people; my family was once again having New Years dinner. I made my way downstairs, showered and sat at the table. I was crashing hard, like a rocket ship falling from the sky in slow motion. My brothers and a couple of the male in-laws were playing a game of street hockey, they were pleading with me to join; after much coercing I went out to play with them. Midway through the game my nose started to bleed profusely. My sinuses were raw from the copious amount of drugs I'd snorted the night before. I wiped my nose on my sleeve and laughed to myself, "Rusty pipes."

I reconnected with D', he had made some pretty trite music with an older girl that had hung out in Denver's goth scene. I understood that D' needed to make music, just as I had to make art. But the material he created with others was subpar and clichéd. I missed singing, I had toyed with other bands but they all lacked the fire I had captured with D'; together D' and I were what we could never be apart. Creatively, D' needed me as much as I needed him.

I apologized for abandoning him. D' and I made up and began hanging out, toying with new tracks and practicing some old songs. D' seemed impressed with the progress I'd made with my voice, I could shift between a throaty snarl, like a revving motorcycle engine and swerve toward crooning melodies. I decided the material we were working on would also be called Divine Reich. I conceived Divine Reich as not simply a band, but a social movement; a safe place for anyone of any gender, sexuality, race or class to dance and party. I wanted the auditory aspect of Divine Reich to be a place for politicians to undress, where society could fall in love and have irresponsible sex. I wanted to bring the world to my level. We'd evolve society by any means necessary. If outsiders took issue with our manifesto of well-intended partying and societal evolution, we'd destroy them, evolution and enlightenment by any means necessary. We'd kill them before they attacked us. We created an LLC, acting as a makeshift record label and management company so we could release music under our own power.

It was springtime and my creativity was thriving in the warm air and budding flowers. D' and I wrote a handful of new tracks. I loved sitting at my desk at the college, drawing all afternoon, into the evening and then rushing to the recording studio and writing songs and laying down vocals.

I existed on a diet of candy, fruit and tea. I channeled all my energy into art and music. D' and I were both fans of Prince, he had once created an opposite gender alter ego for himself. I loved the idea of an alter ego, responsible for everything scandalous we'd say, do or create. Prince had since embraced stifling religion and was now incapable of such base creative brilliance, so D' and I gave his alter ego a home in our heads. We began referring to any and all of our bad behavior as something done by a genderless creature named Camille. Camille loved to dance; her favorites were slow, sleazy songs. Camille became a very real, if not very troubled individual, sharing our lives and our baser tendencies.

Those were good days. D' and I were like brothers again, forgetting all the reasons we grew apart. Jolene was still around, but I'd grown up a bit and learned to deal with her specific neuroses.

I had become close with a girl at the college named Melissa; she was a fine art student. Melissa and I seemed to share an immediate bond, knowing when one of us was thinking of the other and usually exactly what the other was thinking. I needed a girl like Melissa in my life. Melissa was the newer, better model of Wendy or Hannah. Melissa was elfin and lovely, with a smirk and scathing wit. Melissa was beautiful like a pixy, but had a violently protective mean streak; she and I became very nearly inseparable.

Jolene was graduating college that May and had a tiny party. I was invited. Jolene's Aunt and some of her other family attended. Jolene's aunt was a native Ethiopian. I was walking through the house, heading to the bathroom. Jolene's aunt was trying to coral a misbehaving child; she was singing to the infant in Ethiopian. The Ethiopian lullaby sounded like a tape being played backwards, it was disarming. Enchanting. I froze in my steps, mesmerized by the aunt's voice and the arresting foreign melody she was singing. For a brief moment I actually liked Jolene, I never would've had that experience without her.

D' and I were both born in June. We planned to host a joint masquerade birthday party at his house outside of Boulder. Divine Reich had become an infamous empire; we left fliers with mysterious, nebulous messages everywhere. The fliers directed recipients to a website that promised the future and flashed slogans that sounded elitist and revolutionary. We intended to write and record enough songs to begin playing shows. I was excited; I was finally creating music I thought was good enough to be proud of. For the first time, nearly every song D' and I co-wrote was at the very least satisfactory, at best they were amazing. In my opinion. We had built up a strong creative synthesis; we enjoyed moments of actual collaborative genius. I couldn't wait to show the world what we were doing.

Our birthdays came and with them our Saturday night masquerade party. D' and I had invited far too many people. To be frank, I did most of the work. I'll be honest, most of the guests came to see *me*, they came to drink and celebrate with *me*. D' brought the usual handful of goth kids he always hung out with. I had invited anyone attractive or smart I'd run across in the months leading up to the party. Melissa came and showered me with gifts. Everyone wore brilliant costumes or masks, or both. My "mask" was thick stage makeup up and down my arms and around my neck, covering my tattoos.

By the end of the night I was showering in front of a handsome lad in D' and Jolene's master bedroom. The lad and I stumbled to D's bed and kissed and groped till Jolene kicked us out, of course. D' overdosed on speed, which we had both taken as a birthday toast, he vomited in front of Jolene. As the sun rose and washed the house in warm, cleansing light, Jolene made me promise not to let D' take drugs ever again. Every possible surface was covered in empty or half full bottles and cans. We had destroyed the house like true rock stars. I agreed to Jolene's demands, knowing D' and I would get high together again sooner or later.

I grew anxious waiting for D' to write new songs, it seemed to take him much longer to create music than it took me to write lyrics and melodies. I was nervous and impatient. I wanted to show the world how talented and fierce we were. D' was moving at a snail's pace and I slowly lost interest in waiting. I had planned to fly to San Diego to attend ComicCon International, an annual exhibition of all things pop culture. All the major comic publishers would be there and I'd get to show my portfolio to famed editors face to face. While D' spun his wheels and made me wait, I drew page after page to show at ComicCon.

Melissa escorted me to the airport on a sunny Wednesday morning in late July; she brought me berries to eat. I had been forgetting to eat and Melissa was taking care of me, she looked after me like a girlfriend. I knew she was attracted to me but I loved her, I wasn't interested in breaking her heart or wrecking her life. I needed her more than a temporary relationship would allow. I flew out to California alone and sat next to a 20-Something year old skater using an Osiris backpack as a carryon. I loved Osiris. I knew that skater was my date for the flight.

My brief airport association with that skater set the tone for my stay in California. I was dangerous alone, left to my own devices I had no outside voice telling me my decisions were ill advised. I rented a car and drove across town to my lodgings. I had booked a room at a luxury hotel in the heart of the city. I enjoyed the opulence of my temporary surroundings. I flew through a few liaisons with native Californians before remembering I was there to show my work. All of this happened within the first day of my arrival in San Diego. I woke early Thursday ready to meet and hopefully charm editors from the biggest comic companies.

I spent Thursday meeting editors and showing my portfolio, I received some valuable advice and one gentleman took photos of my work to take back to New York with him; he was from a small company I had never heard of. I was flattered nonetheless. I decided the rental car was a waste of money and returned it. I hadn't appreciated the vast distance between the rental car drop off and my downtown hotel. I walked alone across most of San Diego, carrying a bag filled with self-promotional materials.

A young man can do a lot of thinking during a death march across a major west coast city. I was nowhere near ready to work for a major publisher, I wasn't disciplined enough. I was arrogant. I wanted to make just a tiny bit more music. I had stories I wanted to tell that any outsider would find mad, irresponsible and irredeemable. I couldn't edit or censor a select few of my cherished ideas and plans. But, I didn't yet deserve to be quite so uncompromising; I didn't have the experience. I hadn't paid my dues. I wanted to stop wasting time with meaningless lovers and self-indulgent nights. I had to; I had too much to do, too much to create.

KALIFORNIA
Photo by Julian Kay

I returned to my hotel and decided to cut my trip short, I wasn't going to work for a big, huge publisher just yet, so there was no reason to be spending hundreds and hundreds of dollars a day in a foreign city. I walked through the gold and marble lobby of my magnificent hotel and stepped into the elevator. The doors closed and I could see myself in the bisected, gilded face of the elevator doors. I looked good, perfectly cropped hair, longer on top and slicked back, vivid tattoos up and down both arms and on my neck, maybe a little thin. Square jaw.

The elevator climbed higher and higher into the sky, it came to a stop on the 7th floor. I stepped off the elevator and stumbled in an introspective daze toward my room, I slid my keycard into to the slit on the door handle and a small light flashed from red to green, allowing me access. I smirked at the innuendo of it all, my room was a prostitute; I was paying a fortune to sleep inside of her every night. A bellhop walked past as I threw my bag to the ground just inside the doorway to my room. I let out a heavy sigh, the bellhop was a young Latin gentlemen. Tall, dark eyes and uniformed like all luxury hotel bellhops. I'm sure there's a fetish for such a thing somewhere: Latin bellhops, there's a fetish for everything. The bellhop locked eyes with me and refused to look away as I stepped backward into my room.

I cocked my head back, licking my dry lips. I wasn't trying to be seductive; I was dehydrated from my walk across the city. I nodded and the bellhop raised his eyebrows, looking quickly from side to side, over each shoulder. He smiled at me and rushed toward me. I closed the door to my room behind him as he stepped inside.

I called my travel agent that night to change my reservations; I would fly out very early the next morning. No one in Denver knew I was returning except Melissa. I hadn't remembered to eat until she asked. I flew back to Denver in a thunderstorm. I hate to fly, the storm added exponential anxiety to my flight. I was seated near the front of the plane and kept my seatbelt fastened for the duration of the flight. The plane was thrown around the sky like a child's ball; the flight crew retreated to the back of the plane and buckled themselves in. I grabbed the wrist of a lovely blonde stewardess as she passed my seat and yanked her close to my face.

"Is this normal?" I demanded reassurance.

"Oh yes, just a bumpy ride." The stewardess tried to reassure me.

I settled back into my seat and felt brave enough to steal one, single glance out a window beside my seat. Lightening flashed in the mid-day sky. I thought about my first visit to California when I was younger. I loved California. I loved the sun, the smell of the air, the heat. I especially loved the heat. I thought about my uninhibited behavior in San Diego. That brief trip sowed the seed for a new project.

What if a man pushed the limits of hedonism, narcissism and self-indulgence to the absolute extreme? What if a man was compelled to give into his basest tendencies, then hated himself for it afterward?

There's more than a little autobiography there, but fictionally, I could push the story as far as it would go. I could do anything. I scribbled a story outline in ballpoint pen on the napkin that had accompanied my complimentary beverage. The story flooded into my head all at once, from start to finish. I knew I would use the concept one day soon, I knew I'd finish the idea. That trip planted the seed that grew into Heaven's Heat Wave, my first graphic novel.

Melissa met me at the airport upon my return to Denver; she brought me green tea and berries, she really did take excellent care of me. I surprised my family with my early return. I didn't tell D' I was back. I had to think about our creative relationship. I would try to remain in hiding throughout the weekend; I needed a break from my life. I wasn't quite ready to be Kristian again. I wrote and sketched all day and then went out to unfamiliar clubs at night, in disguise. It rained. I loved the city in the rain; the sky was covered with a veil, concealing my behavior from the eyes of Heaven. Rain was dramatic. The city suited my aesthetic. In the mist, streets were slick and wet; an oily sheen covered every building. I met a lad named Sean; he kept praising my tattoos, trying to talk to me about punk bands that didn't matter to me. We walked outside the club and kissed in an alley behind the bar, pressing our bodies against each other in the rain.

I returned to my real life promptly on Monday morning. I reconvened with D', I expressed my concerns to him. I told him I was growing impatient and we had to begin playing shows. I was on the verge of losing interest, we had to play shows and illuminate the world with what we were creating as Divine Reich. D' brought his friend Eddie into the band. Eddie was nicknamed Spigger; Eddie was allegedly half black and half Mexican, thus the nickname.

Eddie was an enthusiastic psychobilly, a rockabilly-gone-wild. D' made Eddie our bassist. In all the years I had known D' he was incapable of finding a drummer or keyboardist to support us live. It would be D', Eddie and I onstage. I made arrangements to play the Church on Halloween night; that would be our big coming out party. We'd return to the place we played our first show as the New Gods and play as Divine Reich. We'd unveil better material and a tighter skill set. I couldn't wait.

D' and I wrote and recorded a song called Hardkore; the song included samples from George Lucas' THX1138, a movie we both worshipped. We took Hardkore to the Church one Sunday night for a preview reveal, the dance floor filled with people writhing to the melody. The song was about a young lad I was obsessed with at the time, the break in the song repeated the year of his birth over and over again: one-nine-eight-four. It was a violent, obsessive love letter to someone I had a crush on. The audience moved with the song.

My then current iteration of Divine Reich went out with Eddie's girl April and Jolene for Labor Day, the five of us went to the Church for some band mate team building and dancey-gothy fun. D' and I were looking for the same thing, a creative outlet we could trust. We were looking for a band that would function like a street gang: dangerous, rebellious, revolutionary, and protective.

We quickly spiraled out of control, the Church was packed to capacity and we stormed through the shoulder-to-shoulder crowd shoving dancers from our path and knocking people down. Once we finished our drinks we threw the empty glasses into the crowd. The singer D' had worked with between stints working with me was there; she was older but dressed like a girl in her twenties. We watched as she danced, throwing lit matches at her. We were the boys of Divine Reich and we were a cyclone of destruction. I was the leader of the pack and I wanted my lieutenants rabid and running wild. We left the Church and headed back to our car. There was a Mustang blocking our parking spot. D' and I smashed rocks into the Ford, denting the car's body. Nobody trapped the boys from

Divine Reich in their parking spot. The nerve. We went to a private after party at yet another decommissioned Church, this one renovated into a living space. Church's were a recurring theme for us.

The first floor of this second Church was a huge greeting area, with the main party occurring on the second floor. D' and I went to the bathroom together and took my last bit of speed, then rejoined the party, loud music, pleasure seeking and depravity. The night wound down and we left, D' was too intoxicated to drive and I was too tall for the back seat. Minutes into our drive D' got sick; he spent the ride home vomiting on the floor of his own backseat.

D' hired a local photographer for our first official shoot, the photographer met us at a seedy motel off of Colfax, an area renowned for it's population of street level hookers. The room we rented at the dilapidated motel was staged appropriately; the photographer took a few merely okay photos of the band before fixating on Eddie's pregnant wife. Eddie's wife April was beautiful and punk rock; she deserved the attention, but we had paid the photographer to shoot *us*, not April. Wonderful April could hire her own photographer. I was less than enthused and even more horrified when I saw the outcome of the photo shoot; we had only one or two usable pictures. The rest were tripe. The photographer was a hack. I could have shot those photos myself, with a disposable camera. I chalked it up to another bad decision on D's part, hiring a subpar, amateurish photographer.

I practiced with D' and Eddie as Divine Reich for a few months, Halloween approached. Eddie came up with some very enthusiastic ideas; he had *very nice* ideas. Clearly I'd use none of them. Eddie was a basement punk rocker and a three-chord garage musician. Eddie was a good guy; I just didn't want be on stage with him. Eddie was D's hire, not mine.

I knew this iteration of Divine Reich wouldn't last. I had used the name I created as a working title for a band I didn't want to be in anymore. I had hinted to D' about my desire to fire or replace Eddie, D' sent me flowers in hopes of swaying me. I went to see P.J. Harvey with friends. After the P.J. Harvey show, D' and Jolene met me at Charlie's, the gay cowboy bar, and we discussed the state of Divine Reich. I told them I didn't want Eddie in the band. Eddie was a great guy, he just wasn't good enough to play my songs or stand next to me onstage. Fundamentally, Eddie didn't fit my aesthetic.

I dissolved Divine Reich. I walked away from my admittedly brilliant collaborative relationship with D' once again. Oh well, thus the cost of artistic integrity.

I was in my twenties, thin as fuck, had a square jaw, striking European good looks, charisma and charm. The world was mine.

I had plans on Halloween night to go clubbing. I was going as myself, I was tired of masks. Evening approached and I felt a touch of agoraphobia setting in; I didn't want to be around crowds of people. A young blonde lad named Steve contacted me; we never exchanged last names or personal information, I only knew him as Steve. I referred to him as Steve X. Steve found me online and I made arrangements to meet him in a hotel parking lot. Steve X was the All-American, blonde, boy next door; he was hot-as-fuck. Steve X had no obvious brain nor any noticeable ambition, but again, he was hot-as-fuck. I soon discovered Steve X had the ability to cause a feverish state of arousal within me. For Steve X, I was a dog in heat. I don't how he did it, maybe pheromones. We started to drive around the neighborhood surrounding the hotel. Steve X went down on me, when I ejaculated he opened the car door as we drove and spat my DNA onto the street. That's how I spent Halloween night.

13, THE INVISIBLE KING
Photo by Agent Lain

Chapter 22: ACTION OF THE TIGER

I began going out alone, cruising the city for adventure. Like a ravenous vampire, I eased down the city's moonlit streets, slinking from club to club. I was much more dangerous by myself, my conscience was non-existent. I could fall in love; I could have as much sex as I wanted, wherever I wanted. I could live new lives; I could destroy those lives the second I became bored. I proceeded with work on a second Divine Reich comic book, which I planned to self publish. I spent a lot of time with Melissa; she was brilliant. Melissa was the perfect second in command: passionate, creative and protective. Melissa loved Japanese youth culture; she was like some obscure anime come to life. Melissa read comics; she was the perfect friend.

On a Sunday night in November Melissa and I went to the Compound to enjoy their high-octane drinks before trotting off to the Church for some tragically goth dancing. We were leaving the Compound when I spotted an otherwise unassuming dark haired lad wearing a Green Lantern shirt. No one ever wore comic book shirts to gay clubs then. Comics had always been my secret language. As a child the world of comics was the place I could escape to when school bullies or my family became too intense. I spent much of my childhood alone in my bedroom, dreaming four-color dreams. The young man, this Green Lantern, wasn't impossibly handsome, he was just an ordinary guy, but it was so rare to see a guy wearing any kind of comic book related clothing. I had to talk to him.

I approached the Green Lantern and complimented his shirt; I referred to him as Hal, the Green Lantern's secret identity. The Green Lantern's face lit up at my words, he knew we spoke the same secret language. Our eyes locked; there was palpable tension between us, like a superhero and his arch villain suddenly deducing their alter egos in a busy nightclub. I handed the Green Lantern my phone number and left with Melissa.

Thanksgiving was the following week, I celebrated with Jacques and his wife; we drank so much wine before dinner my saliva was dark burgundy. The next day I received a text message from the Green Lantern; his name was Jarod. I met Jarod at a coffee shop and showed him some of my illustration work; he seemed impressed and showed me a rough black and white comic he wrote as an advertisement for the club he worked for. Jarod was a service industry guy; he worked at a club, his dad was just a dad that worked in a warehouse, his mom was just a mom. Jarod and I were from different worlds.

It had been so long since I interacted with someone who wasn't an extremist, a bohemian artist or a wanton rebel; I had to relearn how to be human. I had to force myself to remember what it was like to be one of the masses. My excitement for Jarod turned to adoration, we began dating. Kissing Jarod made me remember I had a heart, being with him made me happy. We could talk about the X-Men or Batman and then fall asleep in each other's arms. My heart raced every time I'd receive a message from Jarod during my long hours at work, when we weren't together I couldn't wait to see him. Jarod worked at the newest iteration of Tracks. I'd hang out in the club while Jarod worked, dancing and having infrequent cocktails; I didn't really drink while we dated. I didn't use drugs at all. When the bar closed, I'd wait till Jarod cleaned up and take him home. I would have never thought myself interested enough to sit and wait for my boyfriend, but for Jarod I was patient. I would sit inside the empty club as the staff cleaned, I'd watch Jarod work and smile. Just being around him, just being physically close to him was enough. I was falling in love.

Melissa hated Jarod; she considered him a pedestrian that didn't deserve to be with me. Melissa thought I was talented and special, she thought Jarod was just blue-collar cannon fodder; he had no future. Melissa was a vicious, violent tiger, willing to dismember anything that threatened her. My relationship with Jarod threatened my friendship with Melissa and she stood ready to pounce on him at any second. Jarod would sleep at my house, in my bed. In the morning, if my family was over, I'd introduce them to the boy I was in love with. They all said Jarod wasn't my type. Our relationship was intense, we'd make love in cars, he'd push me up against the wall in elevators and we'd lose ourselves in one another, kissing passionately. We'd separate and smooth out our clothes in time for the doors to open for other riders. He brought me flowers at work. We fought. We were both jealous and possessive. Jared would scan the crowd at Tracks for me while he worked, making sure I wasn't with anyone else.

I never cheated on Jarod. Ever.

On Christmas Eve we exchanged gifts, we were both excessive with the presents we gave one another, like most young hearts in love are prone to do. Jarod gave me graphic novels and action figures. It was pretty cool, having a boyfriend who understood my pop culture obsessions. The last gift Jarod gave me was a little purple card, he had written, "I love you" inside. That was the first time his feelings for me were verbalized. Jarod told me he loved me on a bright Christmas Eve.

I met Jarod's family that afternoon; I celebrated Christmas Eve with his mother, father and extended family. Jarod came from a pretty traditional Hispanic family; he was afraid to tell his parents he was gay for fear of losing them. They all thought I was just their son's white, tattooed friend. I assumed by his mother's scowl and suspicious, accusatory gaze that she knew the truth about her son and I; she knew we were *together*. Once again, I could never have imagined caring about anyone else's family enough to spend a holiday with them. After all, Jarod's dad was just a dad who worked in some warehouse; his mom was just a mom and someone's wife. They were nothing like me or my family; they were a different species. They didn't have pet lions and tigers, and his father wasn't a monstrous war hero. His mom wasn't an angel like mine. I felt awkward and uncomfortable around these commoners and pedestrians, I didn't know how to treat them; I didn't know how to converse with them.

Toward the end of the celebration a cake was brought out and candles were lit. They all sang Happy Birthday to Jesus. It was one of the most surreal moments of my life.

I spent New Years Eve alternating between Jarod and Melissa. I went to Melissa's favorite club with her and then rushed to the heart of the city to meet Jarod. He was on the 16th street mall with 100,000 other people, all of them waiting for the fireworks display that would usher in the New Year. Jarod was with a friend of his; they planned to film the fireworks. The streets of Denver were packed with partying revelers.

Jarod and I ran away from the dense crowd just before midnight. Jarod pulled me after him as he ducked into a recessed alcove on the façade of a building. He wanted to be alone with me for just a second. Fireworks exploded over our heads and the nearby crowd screamed. Jarod and I kissed as the New Year began.

We were young and in love. We were superheroes.

I hated that Jarod worked in a club, I wanted him to be more than that, and I needed *him* to want to be more than that. My boyfriend had to be more than a bartender. I used some of my contacts to get him hired at a comic store. I thought he could work at the comic store and work on his writing and filmmaking, two things he loved. It wasn't the solution, but a step in the right direction. I wanted Jarod to jettison his pedestrian friends and become something like me.

My mum made a comment about Jarod one morning that cut me to the core; she said, "What are you doing with him? All he'll ever do is run alongside you, trying to keep up."

I was trying to force Jarod to evolve and he resisted. I loved him, I did, but I knew I'd love him so much more if he could evolve into one of my kind. I hated myself for my dissatisfaction with Jarod's life; I told myself his love should be enough. I knew it wasn't. We had been dating for a few months and I realized it wasn't going to work out. I was a Space Vampire and he was a civilian. His possessive behavior was suffocating me and I started to become interested in other people. A couple of attractive, faceless pedestrians approached me at Tracks one night and one of them asked for my number, he was young and curious and he thought I looked tough and hot. They were just kids, it was meaningless. Jarod became enraged and accused me of seducing them, like I had sent a psychic summons across the club and made them come after me. Jarod was sure I was going to sleep with one of the boys behind his back. I couldn't take it anymore; I just wasn't designed to be anybody's boyfriend.

I called Jarod from work one afternoon and asked if we could just be friends. Jarod refused, he said that wasn't what he wanted. I told him I'd stop by Tracks that night. I talked to Melissa, she of course advised me to drop him like a ton of bricks. I walked into Jarod's club alone and ended our relationship with one, single sentence. I left, speeding toward Melissa, who waited for me at another club nearby. Jarod called my cell phone over and over; I refused to answer, he left voicemails asking me to come back. His voice on the messages was distraught and wrecked, he was pleading with me to talk to him. I could feel my own heart break, just a tiny bit in the back, where no one else could see.

Unfortunately a war of words started between Melissa and Jarod. Melissa had won; I had stayed with her and turned my back on Jarod. Melissa began to gloat and bully Jarod. Jarod was a tough, masculine guy but he let little, tiny Melissa terrorize him. Instead of confronting his true tormentor, Jarod turned on me. Like most lovers, Jarod knew all of my secret weaknesses; he intentionally exploited my most hidden vulnerabilities. I felt my spirit ignite into an awful and familiar, all consuming hatred. My soul burned hotter than ever before. I felt rage burning so hot inside of me that it threatened to consume my very heart and soul, leaving nothing left. I didn't want to eat or sleep; I only wanted to hurt Jarod. I was on fire, burning in constant, perpetual flame. Jarod had unknowingly set my worst side free. Once again I was burning up. It's true; I really *do* have the worst temper.

Melissa and I launched an entirely unnecessary tragic campaign against Jarod, some of which is too terrible to relate here. Melissa and I, in the spirit of self-preservation and mutual survival, were capable of such shocking acts of violence and aggression that it scared me. The campaign culminated in our burning of every present Jarod had given me for Christmas on the hood of his car parked outside Tracks. He had used his hard earned, blue-collar money to buy me gifts and I was burning them in defiant effigy, it was like a cremation. I allowed Melissa to take a Polaroid of the purple card as it burned in my hand; the card where Jarod had written, "I love you". The club security looked on in amazement as Melissa and I created a funeral pyre on the hood of Jarod's car, sending what I thought was a pretty clear message.

If I couldn't love Jarod, I'd destroy him. I left nothing standing; I attacked Jarod on every front. Scorched Earth mentality.

Jarod had me banned from Tracks. Melissa and I were both dressed in solid white and intended to hear a friend of ours DJ for the final time at Tracks before he moved on. I was on the guest list. Before Melissa and I stepped foot inside the club, uniformed police and the club's collective security force met us at the door. We were told that Jarod was afraid for his safety and that we had been banned from Tracks for life. Melissa and I left in a fit of laughter and went everywhere else in the city, anywhere with loud music, a bar and a dance floor.

My behavior was immature and vicious, but Jarod *knew* I was a monster. Jarod knew I was intense and passionate. He chose to capitalize on my fears and weaknesses; nobody does that, even if I love them. Especially if I love them.

Jarod knew I was a tiger and one shouldn't be surprised when their pet Tiger *acts* like a Tiger and mauls them.

The weeks and months that followed were some of the wildest and most uninhibited of my entire life. I had become obsessed with finishing the Divine Reich comic I was working on; I worked feverishly on the story and art. I began to use dangerous quantities of drugs. I spiraled out of control and I loved it, I loved the dizzying blur of days and nights. I was under weight and Melissa constantly had to remind me to eat. We went out nearly every night, Melissa stayed at my house when we took the party too far, which happened very often.

On the rare nights when I wasn't out running wild with Melissa I would stay up till dawn, drawing pages for Divine Reich. I decided I'd call the book Divine Reich: Love Is The Devil, because it was. My recent past and all those boys had proven how terrible a thing love was.

I was the king of the city, night's bringer of chaos and lust, the twilight's avatar of abandon. I was living the life of a bohemian artist and loved every second of it all. Melissa was my second in command; we were fierce tigers prowling the city like a jungle catwalk, waiting to unsheathe our claws.

Melissa and I went out on a lovely Thursday night. I spent the early part of the evening at my day job, drawing pages for Love Is The Devil. Thursday was one of the best nights to go out in Denver. I never knew why, but the streets of the city were filled with late night revelers. Any night I went out with Melissa, or 'Lissa as I affectionately referred to her, was a night pregnant with dangerous possibilities. 'Lissa and I went to the Compound for a starter cocktail and then headed to JR's for another.

JR's was a multi-level gay bar on 17th Street, the interior looked like an old plantation house. Crowded and well lit, at JR's you could actually see whom you were flirting with.

Melissa and I were in her car, driving up 17th street toward JR's. A young gentleman was walking down the street placing fliers for a show or club on the windshields of parked cars. Melissa and I stopped at an intersection and the young man tried to hand Melissa a flier, he said, "You should check this out!"

Melissa dismissively said, "No thanks."

The young man tossed a flier into the sun roof above our heads and I barked, "What the fuck?!"

When Melissa said she didn't want a flier, she meant it. Disregarding traffic, Melissa pulled out of the intersection, speeding after the young man in an attempt to run him down. Chasing after the poor, terror-stricken fellow, Melissa drove over curbs and on sidewalks in an effort to punish him for littering in her car. The young man lost us by running between parked cars. 'Lissa and I abandoned our pursuit and parked, nonchalantly walking into JR's as if running someone down was an everyday occurrence.

After a drink or two 'Lissa and I headed to the bathroom, I was channeling Sid Vicious and spat on a pool table as we passed. The group of twinks playing pool took great offense to my punk rock posturing and we had a heated exchange culminating in me shattering my glass against one of their chests.

Melissa and I were involved in yet another altercation with a twink named Eric; he asked if I was Jarod's boyfriend. Eric's question sent Melissa and I into a murderous fury. We followed Eric to Charlie's where we shoved him as we passed through the crowd. Eric was brave enough to talk back to us; Melissa ran after him and pushed him to the ground before he could get out of the club. The staff and uniformed police happily stood by, watching and laughing as Melissa assailed Eric's cringing form with kicks, punches and stomps. I loved that girl.

'LISSA AND I DURING THE WAR
Photo by Agent Lain

I was nearly finished with Love Is the Devil and realized I was hurting Melissa with every moment we spent together. I was allowing her to hope for the eventuality of an impossible relationship with me. I desperately needed her as a friend, but she wanted more. I knew Melissa wanted to be Mrs. 13. I decided I'd push her away; I was trying to save her. I told Melissa frankly that she would never be my girl; I'd never return her romantic feelings for me. She was furious and refused to speak to me on any level, for any reason.

I was back to cruising the city alone, looking for adventure. I had numerous exploits that spring. I revved my engine and spun my wheels like a racecar at the starting line, having affairs with a punk rock bartender named Frank and a flame-throwing lad named Zane. I dated them both because of their Mohawks.

D' had proposed to Jolene and asked me to be in their wedding party. I'd have to fly to Alabama or somewhere else I didn't care about to participate; I can't really recall the exact location. I agreed and met up with the happy couple to be measured for our tuxedos. I thought about the wedding and called D' to tell him I wouldn't be able to stand up for him. I couldn't stand beside D' as one of his "best men" and watch him marry Jolene. Not only did I feel overwhelming ambivalence toward Jolene, I also thought marriage itself was passé. Stupid.

A dress and a party won't make two people stay together. A piece of paper and some rings won't make me love someone.

I had finally begun to slow down after long, extreme months of work and play. I knew I had to decelerate or risk burning out. I was acting out violently and behaving too self indulgently, I was afraid of overdosing, or killing myself or someone else. I knew I had to find something outside of myself to help me direct my energy. I began to take copious amounts of martial arts classes at the only studio in Denver that offered traditional Japanese Karate. The sensei, a middle aged Japanese man, was a martial arts badass but appeared perpetually serene and at peace. I went to him to teach me humility, to temper my rage and teach me how to focus my energy. In Sensei's studio, I had to submit and I had to show respect. That training helped me clear my head and calm myself after my recent perpetual eruptions.

The spring ended with the release of Love Is The Devil. I had written the story myself, I had drawn every single panel. It was my very first full-length attempt at visual story telling. In true punk rock fashion, I printed 1,500 copies of the book on the college's printers. A perk of my day job; I would stay on campus alone until 3 or 4 am after closing the buildings and use the school's high quality facilities to print books. I'd practice the kata Sensei had taught me in darkened and abandoned halls of my college, while hundreds of pages printed. I'd trim the pages to comic size, fold each page into book form and then bind them together by hand. 1,500 copies. Cut, folded and bound by hand. Divine Reich: Love Is The Devil was truly a grassroots indie book. I was doing it all my way. Punk–fucking-rock.

I made sure Love Is The Devil was finished, printed, announced and released in April. The month I finished college, the month my father died.
D' helped me with a website design and I marketed the book on my own, selling the print run out completely within a few months.

Summer, my birthday and Pride Fest were all approaching. I had made up with Melissa and we were trying to enjoy a strictly platonic friendship. I was invited to a huge Pride party held in a penthouse apartment overlooking the city. The party would spill out onto the roof of the building. I invited Melissa and Chrissy Espinoza, a mutual college friend to attend with me. The evening was mad fun; we drank and posed in a penthouse. The girls and I were sitting on a couch in the penthouse's living room. Another guest approached us and asked our names. Without missing a beat Melissa, Chrissy and I all responded with pseudonyms.

Melissa brought her very replaceable boyfriend along, he was slightly homophobic and unaware that the party was hosted and mostly attended by gay men. We were watching the sunset over the city from the rooftop, Melissa and I decided to head inside for another drink. Her boyfriend wanted to stay outside. As we walked away, a clique of twinks approached him shouting, "Hey girl!"

It was at that rather comical moment that Melissa's boyfriend realized he had come to a gay party; they were broken up by the next morning.

Jeremy and I made plans to attend the pride parade and rally the next day, as was tradition. Jeremy was hours late to meet me in the morning. I knew he had visited a dealer to acquire drugs. We sped to the rally and took turns taking bumps of cocaine from a small compact; Jeremy always hid his drugs in his makeup. We laughed about the metaphoric powdering of our noses. Jeremy and I ran around all day, snorting cocaine in the boiling summer heat. We had fun. That was the last time I saw Jeremy; he just faded away.

Chapter 23: SEDUCTION OF THE INNOCENT AND THE AMERICAN GIGOLO

I was packing for a trip to California when I received a phone call from a lad named Benjamin. At that time, Benjamin was an illustration student at the college I'd attended. Benjamin also loved comics, just like me. Our similarities ended there. Benjamin was a humorous and charming young man, but he lacked work ethic and ambition and had only the tiniest understanding of accountability. Benjamin lived off of his divorced parents like an heiress; a big spoiled baby in an adult's body. Benjamin was a thick cocktail of Latin and Caucasian, a well-muscled oaf of a boy. Benjamin lived to work out, collect music and comics and have a good time. Benjamin was unsophisticated; he was raw, undeveloped clay. We had pop culture in common, but Benjamin was the psychological and emotional antithesis of myself. I liked him from the start; he was like a pet, my pet gorilla.

Benjamin had called me seeking my advice on a disastrous and damaging relationship he had gotten involved in. A relationship he had been dismissed from. Benjamin had fallen in love with and been dismissed by a much younger guy. I tried my best to help Benjamin through the heartbreak during that initial phone call; our conversation cemented a close and resilient friendship between the two of us.

Benjamin and I became best friends and brothers, I snuck him into his first gay club before he turned 21, a strip club no less. Ben's eyes grew wide as the dancers gyrated on-stage; I had introduced him to my world. We began to hang out and for the first time I had a best friend who wasn't out of his mind with intentionally destructive behavior. Ben was indeed destructive, but never *intentionally*. I was standing at the urinal in a club one night and Ben came in looking for me, accidently ripping the bathroom door off its hinges in excitement. The things Ben broke or the people Ben hurt were only damaged because of his enormous size and power, Benjamin was a hulking brute who didn't comprehend his own strength. Benjamin was my pet monkey, my Frankenstein monster. Benjamin was Beast Man to my Skeletor.

Belying his size and strength, Benjamin was also a big baby, a sensitive and fragile soul; he had the power to crush a man's skull but he'd cry if you punched him in the arm. Benjamin was Superman. I was Batman. Ben was optimistic and a touch naïve. I was brooding and jaded. We were the World's Finest crime fighting duo.

As brothers, I exposed Benji to many adventures; after turning 21 he became a fixture in my nightclub life. He'd sing along to songs being played at JR's, screeching like bad karaoke and attracting the wrong kind of attention. I'd shove him, telling him to shut his mouth. I ordered him to stand and posture in silence as we drank. Pose for the eyes of the masses. I taught Benjamin how to be cool.

I met a pleasant, all-American looking lad at JR's who asked to fellate me. I'm never one to disappoint an admirer, so we retired to the men's room where the young man and I locked ourselves in a stall. I left Benjamin outside unattended. The all-American lad went down on me and I closed my eyes and laid my head back, enjoying his efforts. Long moments passed and I felt my skin tingle, I was on the verge of rewarding the young man with a strand of rare and coveted pearls. Suddenly I heard Benji's voice.

"Kristian?" Benji's disembodied voice whispered.

I opened my eyes in surprise and saw no one in the stall with my new friend and I. I dismissed the sound, closing my eyes once again. Perhaps I was hearing things, I reasoned.

"Kristian!" Benji's voice whispered again, but was much more insistent this time.

I opened my eyes to see Benji's smiling face over the top of the divider between my stall and the next; he had entered the bathroom and was standing on the toilet in the stall beside mine. Benji was whispering in hopes of getting my attention, but softly as to not disturb the young lad diligently sucking my cock. Oh, Benji. I looked Benjamin in the eyes and smiled at him, raising my eyebrows.

"Hurry, okay? We've gotta go!" Benjamin said, tapping the invisible watch on his wrist.

I nodded with a smirk and tapped the all-American lad's shoulder forcefully.

"Hurry up." I commanded.

I ejaculated and made the lad give me his underwear as a souvenir of the night.

That set a trend for Benji and I; I often gave him ringside seats to the circus of depravity that was my everyday life.

SHARING A MOMENT WITH BENJI
Photo by Camille

Love Is The Devil had been a success, so I began work on another indie book. I planned to call the book Seduction Of The Innocent, an empowering title appropriated from a book written by the awful Fredric Wertham, a terrible and paranoid "crusading psychiatrist" who launched a witch-hunt against comic books in the 1950's. Crazy old Wertham directly blamed comic books for juvenile delinquency, rape and murder. Wertham's witch-hunt culminated in senate hearings where he testified against the life ruining and mind altering depictions of sex, drug use and violence in comics. I thought it was very appropriate to name my next book after the work of a man who neutered my best-loved art form; my work would surely feature all the things Wertham railed against.

I intended Seduction Of The Innocent to be an anthology; it'd be a handful of short stories. Benjamin and a couple other friends were invited to submit a drawing that would appear on the inside front and back cover.

The more I got to know Benjamin the more I realized he was an empty glass of identity that he filled with the ideas, interests and personality traits of others. I assumed everything I learned about Benji was sampled from another source, another friend or role model. As Benji and I spent time together, he started to absorb parts of me; Benjamin was stealing my glow. Benjamin had no ideas of his own. Intentionally or otherwise, Benjamin stole music, hobbies, opinions and affect from me. I would have hated anyone else for appropriating my thoughts and words, but Benji was a project, a fixer upper. I allowed him to program himself with a Kristian Identity-Disk, but I kept the most cherished aspects of my personality under lock & key, refusing to share them.

I repeated the routine I had established while writing Love Is The Devil; I'd arrive at the college in the early afternoon to work my day job. I'd steal as many hours as I could to draw pages for Seduction Of The Innocent at my desk. Then I'd either go out with Benji or go home and keep drawing.

Benji was a bassist and we often discussed music, he'd magically fall in love with most of the bands that I referenced as a fan or inspiration. I began to keep things from him; I refused to allow Benjamin access to the core of my spirit. I wanted something left for myself and I knew Benji would absorb everything about me if I let him. I wanted my most loved things to remain secret and special. I refused to allow Ben to siphon the totality of my identity; he could only have a little. A little was all he could handle.

I was working on scanning pages of art for Seduction one night near the end of winter when my side began to itch. I thought I had a tag in my clothes that was irritating my skin. As the night progressed, so too did the irritation. I had a headache. By the time I went home, I felt sick and my side was on fire. I woke up the next day with excruciating pain on my right side and a pattern of furiously red, raised bumps on my hip in the shape of a helix. I saw Doctor Gale, who quickly quarantined me from the other patients in his office and ran some tests. Doctor Gale swiped a cotton swab across my side, the swab's touch felt like white-hot flames shooting up the right side of my body. He sealed the swab in a vial and sent it to a lab.

I was diagnosed with Shingles, an adult reactivation of a childhood bout with Chickenpox that I don't remember having. Doctor Gale told me I was terribly contagious. I laid a sheet over my couch and tried to rest. The infection was surprisingly painful, much more so than of the tattoos I'd received on my arms, legs, chest and neck. Agonizing.

The fact that I wasn't eating regularly, staying out all night, partying without conscience and working myself too hard probably didn't help my health.

My body slowly fought off the infection and I went about life. I finished Seduction Of The Innocent and printed it in the same manner as Love Is The Devil, using the college's facilities in secret, in the ghostly hours before dawn.

I asked the wonderful DJ's at Lipgloss, at the time Denver's premier nightclub, to host a release party for Seduction Of The Innocent. Lipgloss was enjoying national media attention in entertainment and lifestyle magazines; it was the perfect place to debut my new book. I printed huge, 6-foot posters of Seduction's cover and a few interior pages and hung them throughout the club; I wanted guests to literally walk through the story. I had toy guns with my web address on them and buttons with art from the book made; the buttons featured two boys kissing. I laid the guns and buttons out on tabletops inside the club. Limited edition t-shirts with my art on them were sold at the party.

Benji was there as my most trusted Lieutenant; Chrissy Espinoza came to help work the merchandise booth. The club filled to capacity as soon as the doors opened at 9pm. There was a perpetual line of guests, waiting to get in. Jacques and his wife came with some childhood friends. Several associates and acquaintances attended. However, my favorite attendees were the ones I'd never met before. A mob of people came that I'd never previously seen; my shameless self-promotion had worked. I had carefully planned the entire event. I promoted the party through all available venues: fliers, website and social media. I was still a tiny bit surprised when so many people showed up, buying books and drinks and t-shirts. I was asked to sign copies of Seduction of the Innocent as they were purchased, I was asked for autographs. It was an amazing night.

Do you know what all the kids that bullied me in grade school were doing at the time? No? That's okay; neither does any one else. This story has a moral: kids who get spit on grow up to sign autographs.

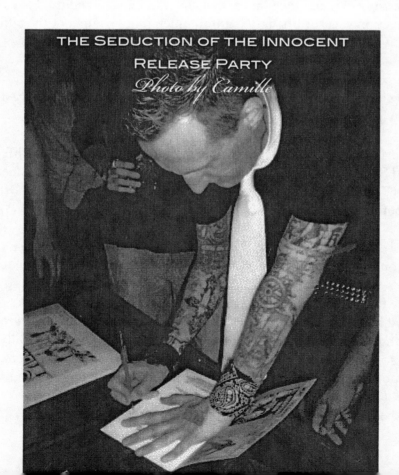

THE SEDUCTION OF THE INNOCENT
RELEASE PARTY
Photo by Camille

Another victory to be cherished, another night that made my wild and wicked life seem worthwhile. The Seduction of the Innocent release party was held in April, the same month I graduated college and later released Love is the Devil. The same month my father died.

D' showed up to the Seduction release party with Jolene, I introduced him to Ben. D' and I began discussing Divine Reich and the songs we'd written together. We agreed that those songs deserved a chance to be heard. I signed a tongue-in-cheek agreement with D' on a cocktail napkin, we agreed to finish an album. I had a plan regarding Divine Reich. I told D' we'd resume writing and work to finish an album at the end of the summer.

Benjamin had begun dating a guy named Jerry, from Texas. Jerry was a nice enough fellow, but had the capacity to erupt into irrational, insane behavior. Jerry earned himself the nickname Scary Jerry. Benji and I stopped into a gay strip club one night to heckle the dancers and have a drink before rushing to another club. The bouncer at the door was a short, boxy lad with blonde hair and an all-right face. Not too handsome, but certainly not ugly. I excused myself and walked into the bathroom. The bouncer followed me; he stood next to me at the urinal and asked to see my cock. Dismissing him with a roll of my eyes, I tucked myself back into my shorts and walked out. The bouncer followed me once again.

The bouncer introduced himself as Michael; we exchanged flirtatious words and phone numbers. Benji and I left. By the next day, Michael had posted lengthy blogs online about me; he had detailed his new feelings for me. Michael said he wanted to search the city till he found my car, till he found my home. At first I found Michael's obsessive affection to be charming, perhaps even seductive. We spent time together and had sex in every possible location, offices, public bathrooms, stairwells, parking garages. Whatever.

After awhile, Michael became far too attached; Benji and I re-christened him Psycho Mike-O. I should have paid more attention to his initial obsessive behavior. Michael was desperately trying to find the location of my home, something I kept secret from almost everyone I knew. My home was my Bat-Cave, my hidden Fortress of Solitude. After mistakes with Jason and Jarod, no one was ever going to come to my private home; I need a place to hide and be myself, a place to be anonymous. Michael wouldn't accept that.

Michael called my office one day asking me for a favor. I asked what he wanted and he said, "Come outside."

Michael had found the location of my day job by searching online. I found this neither charming nor flattering, his research and sudden appearance was merely scary and out of control. I went outside to confront Michael and he presented me with a huge bouquet of lilies, which he found out from acquaintances were my favorite flower. I ordered Michael to leave and he burst into tears, making a huge scene for onlookers.

Benji and I were both dating mental cases; best friends share every experience, I guess. Michael confessed to me that he had done porn; he had posed for adult photos. Evidently, Michael had posed for *lots* of adult photos. I didn't care; I had my own experience within the sex industry.

One night before I was to meet up with Benji, I stumbled across some of the photos of Michael online. They were everywhere. Michael was on every website I came across, having sex with other men. The photos were all grainy, haphazard and clumsy; they were amateurish. I hated it. I hated Michael. I couldn't care about someone who proved to be so cheap; loving Michael was most definitely impossible.

I went clubbing with Benji and ignored Michael's text messages; I refused to answer his calls. Michael was obsessively trying to evoke a response, calling uncountable times. I ended up back at Benji's apartment after 2am; I was waiting to sober up. I finally answered Michael's call; I had to tell him he was trash. I had to tell him the photos he had done exceeded my expectations of him as base and common. I ripped him to shreds over the phone.

I was in a state of shock, Michael told me he loved me, but I could see him fucking other men every time I closed my eyes. I was jealous and behaving like a hypocrite. I never wanted any of my lovers to exist before they met me. I wanted anyone I was with to have been created at the second of our introduction and live solely for me. My lovers had been born the moment they met me. Michael ruined that perfect, hypnagogic illusion.

The weeks that followed were intense; I hid from Michael while he launched a desperate search to find my home. I admitted my hypocrisy and apologized and then quickly rescinded my apology, reveling in my hatred. We were engaged in an emotional tug of war. I liked hurting Michael, hitting someone with fists caused bruises, but carefully selected words will cut them and they'll never heal. It was my birthday and Michael began texting me, asking if he could meet me somewhere, anywhere in the city. He said he had something that would change my life. I wasn't sure if he'd try to kill or kidnap me. I agreed to meet him at a coffee shop, when I arrived I saw Michael carrying a happy, light-blue paper gift bag. The bag had a monkey on it with googley eyes, when you moved the bag, the monkey's eyes would go crazy, darting from side to side. That monkey bag is the best part of this story, I assure you.

Michael, insane as ever, refused to give me the bag till we were alone. I agreed to follow him to a nearby park. Once our cars were parked, Michael presented me with cupcakes and finally gave me the bag. My heart sank and filled with dread when I reached inside. Grasping past the tissue, I felt a small box; the kind jewelry is packaged in. I removed the tiny box and opened it, inside was a platinum ring. Michael was trying to propose to me.

I rather stupidly put the ring on my finger; trying it on and watching it gleam in the sun. The platinum ring was just a tiny bit too big on my finger. I realized what was happening and disdainfully removed the ring, handing it back to Michael.

"This doesn't fit and boys can't get married." I said and left.

Michael tried to give me the ring once again, days later, when I was out for a night of stress-free clubbing with Benjamin. I took the ring so Michael would shut up and leave me alone. The next day I threw the ring from my car window as I sped down the highway. I'm nobodies husband, least of all Michael's.

I was once again attending the annual San Diego ComicCon; I had worked on a sardonic Wonder Woman story as a sample to show editors. I invited Benji to be my plus one, my guest. I knew I'd have more fun with my monkey tagging along. I had booked a room in a fabulous hotel on Broadway, in the heart of downtown San Diego. The hotel had been a bank in a previous life, complete with a vault in the basement that now served as a club. I was filled with the usual anxiety during the flight to California; Benjamin helped me remain calm, using his ridiculous sense of humor as a distraction.

We arrived at our hotel and the room was amazing, it included a lovely view of the city and two separate beds. Thank god. I pushed Benjamin as hard as I pushed myself. I forced Benji to be up early every morning, I wanted to be one of the first artists to present their work to editors looking for new talent, making him trek across the city as the sun rose in order to be among the first to arrive at the convention center. Benji slept like a bear in hibernation; he slept through my wake up call from the front desk, he slept through my shower, he slept through my slamming drawers and talking to him. Finally I resorted to standing on Benji's bed in my underwear and singing David Bowie's "Boys Keep Swinging" at the top of my lungs. Benjamin still wouldn't get up. I knelt down above his persistently sleeping form and pulled my cock from my boxer briefs. I tapped Benji on the top of his head with my dick; the moment he realized what I was slapping him with, he bounced right up. We jokingly referred to my penis alarm clock as pee-pee touching. Pee-pee touching became a metaphor for sexual activity with our numerous respective associates.

I spent the first two days of our trip to San Diego working my ass off, making sure I was in the right place at the right time to meet the right industry mogul or editor. I made some decent connections and met some quite brilliant men and women. After that second straight day of work it was time to unwind and enjoy the city, I love the west coast. Benji and I went shopping like teen-age girls with an unlimited budget. There was another catch phrase born on that trip: "Teen Age Girling"; literally meaning to behave like a rabid capitalist, snatching up everything in sight. The phrase references the 1980's cliché of the mall-faring teen girl. Such fun. We went to an amazing skate shop in downtown San Diego called Street Machine where we both spent a small fortune.

A mutual friend of ours named Vern drove up from Los Angeles. Originally we planned to drive back to L.A. for the night but things didn't work out that way. Benji and I dressed for clubs and asked the concierge where a lad could get a drink in San Diego. It helped that the concierge was gay with a capital G; he listed a few bars and clubs in proximity of each other. We ran from club to club, drinking and watching go-go dancers move badly to the music. It was nice to see that the phenomenon of beautiful men with no rhythm being paid to flail around spastically was national, not limited to Denver.

I was walking through the club, surveying the trade when I made eye contact with a young Latin guy; he began to follow me. We cruised each other like sharks. I stopped midway down a long, darkened hallway. Flickering strobe lights illuminated our faces in short, flashing bursts. The Latin guy reached into my pants and began to stroke my dick. I didn't stop him, I was a tourist and I wanted to see the sights.

Benjamin approached and interrupted the rather public display of anonymous affection. Benji said, "Hey, we've gotta go. Vern wants to check out another club!"

I straightened out my clothes and left the hand job I was receiving half finished. After visiting a few more bars, we returned to the hotel and separated. I went to my room with Vern; I invited him to sober up on our floor. Benji stayed in the lobby, pacing the floor while he spoke to Scary Jerry over the phone. I abandoned Vern to the floor of the hotel room and went for a walk. Vern had passed out and I needed some air. Vampires always roam the city late at night. It was 2am, the bars were closed and the streets were filled with bad ideas and intoxicated minds. The next day Benjamin confronted me about what I had done. The concierge told Benji I had returned to the hotel with a guest, I had brought a trick back with me. I assumed Benji was jealous. The concierge was lying; I didn't bring a trick back with me. Not to my room, anyway.

The lobby of that hotel was beautifully cavernous. I didn't need to take anyone back to my room.

Benji and I returned to Colorado on a flight so turbulent that my anxiety was contagious. By the time our plane landed in Denver we were both frazzled and panicking. I contacted D' and we began to ease back into a working relationship, writing new songs and perfecting the few we'd previously been toying with.

Benji and I were out one Sunday night, running from the Compound to the Church. A very handsome lad began to follow me around the Church. The boy looked painfully out of place, Sunday was strictly goth night. The lad following my every step was dressed like an Abercrombie & Fitch catalogue; 2-Dimensional in a snug black polo shirt with a raised collar and jeans. I wasn't exactly dressed to fit the goth stereotype myself; I'd long ago grown out of the stylistic trappings of genre-based fashion. I think I was wearing perfectly pressed khaki chino shorts, a black skate jersey and a thick bandanna tied around my head, allowing my hair to ascend from the top but mostly obscuring my eyes. I had two full tattooed sleeves; I stood out like an undead skater gone gangster in a sea of pasty skin, crushed velvet and vinyl.

The boy finally approached me and asked for my number. His name was Patrick; he had a beautiful face with large, ultra-expressive eyes. Patrick had a sharp, defined body. Preppy little Patrick was not shy about pulling me close to him and trying to kiss me in the extremely goth, but otherwise straight club. I thought he was cute and brave. I was seeing Patrick romantically within the week; Patrick described his feelings for me as infatuation. Infatuation was acceptable. The first time I had sex with Patrick he ejaculated hands-free while I penetrated him, I was so deep inside of Patrick that he came without touching himself. That visual set a trend; sex with Patrick would last for hours, through multiple orgasms. It was such an amazing sight, I had to tell Benji all about it. Benji and I told each other everything. My relationship with Patrick didn't last. My relationships never lasted. Patrick was another of my associates who turned to porn to make fast money. Patrick said he needed tuition for school and I knew firsthand that fucking him was a remarkable experience. Had it occurred to me, I would've filmed the sex I had with Patrick myself.

Echoing back to my supplemental college income, I would sometimes receive emails or text messages from individuals who were willing to pay for a few moments of my time, men or women willing to buy me for a night. My guilty conscience had subsided and I knew I was very talented at fulfilling fantasies and granting a partner pleasure. I never, ever pursued that lifestyle, but people would come to me assuming I was for sale. Maybe it was word of mouth, maybe I just exuded the air of a Gigolo, and maybe I was just the right fantasy for some people. I never questioned a client's motives.

I established ground rules with clients; I never bottomed, I would never consent to submission. In the *very* expensive event of penetrative sex, I was always the top. I never did anything oral, if a caller wanted to suck my cock that was cool, but there would never be any reciprocation. I would sometimes receive a message while working my legitimate job, asking for my availability. I'd leave work at 10pm and drive to someone's house for a quick fuck. Sometimes I was asked to go to a dark, empty office building after business hours; work was the only discreet place some married men were willing to entertain. They were the bosses there, they spent their days telling others what to do, but now they wanted me to shove them around and own them. Timing and routine sometimes required me to be introduced by clients to their wives, professional colleagues or family as a friend. I was straight acting and appearing, sleeved in tattoos and handsome, no one ever assumed I was gay, and they certainly never assumed I was their husband or boyfriend's sexual partner. I've been paid to receive more fellatio than most men receive in their lifetime. I could seamlessly shift gears and become the caller's fantasy; I was an expert, providing whatever they requested within the predetermined limits. I was their automatic lover.

One of my most memorable clients was a young marine with quarter sleeve tattoos and a luxury apartment paid for by his parents. He'd buzz me into the building and I'd spend an hour towering over him while he worked my cock down his throat. The marine was a recurring client, as he grew comfortable with me, his requests grew more and more desperate and base. The last time the marine bought me, he asked me to meet him in a shadowed alley beside a shopping center. The thrill of exhibitionism and risk of possible discovery aroused the marine. He identified as heterosexual, he couldn't come out of the closet, but he was turned on by the idea of someone catching him as he worshipped another man. We were alone within earshot of busy shoppers; he was on his knees. The marine begged for my cock, pleading for my semen; he wanted someone to be as tough on him as he was on himself.

Benji and I were at JR's one Thursday night when a yuppie in his 30's spotted me and smiled, I had been casually introduced to the yuppie by his business partner, a man with a wife and children. I smirked at him and went on surveying the crowd. The yuppie caught up with me later, while I was walking toward the bathroom with Benji. I felt a foreign hand on my shoulder, gripping me tightly; the yuppie had grabbed me and said, "Give me a call."

The yuppie had handed me a card with a long message scribbled on the back before disappearing back into the crowd. Benji and I went into the bathroom and laughed about the card as we stood side by side at the urinal. Benji stopped laughing when he saw what the guy had written. Along with his name and number the yuppie wrote, "$300 to fuck my ass."

Charming. I knew the guy was into kink, fetishes always cost a little more; $300 wouldn't cover what I knew he wanted. Benji was aware of my activities; he couldn't believe what some callers were willing to pay for. Benji couldn't believe men were willing to pay to suck another man's cock; he just thought it was a mutually beneficial and pleasurable activity. It was never pleasurable for me. It was business.

Chapter 24: DIVINE REICH AND THE LIFE DELUXE

In the coming year, I would experience scenic highs and desolate lows; it would be perfectly typical cinema. I was slaving over new material with D', the hypothetical Divine Reich album was coming into shape as a brilliantly hedonistic and angry electro-rock spectacle.

D' and I were on fire, writing feverishly and enjoying a few moments of genuine synthesis. I had written a song called Resurrection in 2004, D' and I were revisiting the composition. I adored the song and the idea, the lyrical narrative was a literal plea to God for one last chance to be a good man and fall in love.

D' and I recorded Resurrection on a warm night. I was standing in the large, empty foyer of a recording studio with a boom mic set up over my head. We had run cables through the building, from the basement studio and mixing board to my location. I communicated with D' through headphones. The natural echo created by singing in the expansive foyer was perfect; the song was a plea for delivery from isolation. A family was walking down the street outside the studio; they stopped to watch me sing through huge bay windows. The family outside erupted in applause after I had satisfactorily completed and recorded one of the song's choruses. Those were good nights. I was always very happy when I was working.

I'd return home to Golden late at night. This sounds trite, but the twilight hours were magical. I'd have exhausted myself in a recording studio, but Golden always managed to resurrect me. I'd see Foxes and Coyotes walking down my street in plain sight; the animals enjoyed the twilight. Just like me. I pulled into my driveway late one night and heard a loud clacking sound as I stepped out of my car. I turned toward the noise and saw two male deer battling a few scarce yards from my house. Both deer had huge crowns of antlers, with numerous majestic spikes. They looked like kings. The deer butted heads, causing the sound of their conflict to echo through the empty streets. I walked toward their battle in awe. The deer froze as I approached; they both turned my way. I stood motionless and watched as the deer grew bored with me and returned to their fight. I was standing 10 feet from them.

I had decided to name the Divine Reich album *An American Tragedy*, a rather obvious nod to the early 20th Century Theodore Dreiser novel. I loved the book, a story about the American Dream, sex and ultra tragic love; perfect themes for Divine Reich. To further my obsession with the idea, Dreiser's novel was loosely adapted into a film starring Montgomery Clift. Clift was one of the first actors, one of the first men I was ever physically attracted to. The Dreiser book loosely paralleled the album's lyrical content. While my lyrics were set in the 21st Century, the themes ran side by side.

I wanted Benjamin involved in Divine Reich. Originally D' and I were just going to finish and release an album through his new management company. D' was a brilliant businessman and expertly navigated the often treacherous environs of the music industry; he had founded a management company that could act as a record label under which we could release product, allowing us to disseminate our own material. As we worked on newer, stronger songs, we decided it might be a good idea to play shows. Benji was a bassist and I knew he'd follow my orders. Whereas D' and I were both Alpha Males with egos to match, Benji was already my valued Lieutenant. D' was immediately suspicious of Benjamin. During private conversations D' would say that he didn't trust anything Benji said to be original, Benji was a parrot. D' said everything that came out of Benji's mouth was said first by me. D' had Benji's number in that regard. Benji was a follower, a mimic. Benji was a poseur. That was okay, I loved Benji like a brother and we couldn't all be generals.

Benjamin would not be a contributing member of Divine Reich; he would simply be there to play live. I loved the lad, but Benji was a hired gun. Benjamin's involvement in Divine Reich meant I'd have a buffer between D' and I during our frequent, mostly unspoken, passive

aggressive power struggles. Let me clarify that. I *never* struggled with D',
quite the contrary; I enjoyed the most honest, productive and mutually
satisfying creative collaboration with D'. The struggle came with Jolene,
who D' had made the band's manager. Jolene had no experience in the
music industry and no sense regarding song writing or creativity, but
D' made her the co-owner of their fledgling management company and
Divine Reich's manager. I was horrified by what some men were willing to
do just to make sure a body was waiting for them when they return home.

Jolene was a small-time goth girl. I wanted mass exposure, I
wanted to show the entire world what D' and I were making. And I didn't
want to make creative concessions to a layperson. Jolene was just a
girlfriend. Wait, no. At that point Jolene was just a wife.

Thank God for Benji. After band meetings with Jolene, he and
I would go out and make fun of her efforts to verbalize her opinions.
Jolene's repetitious use and theatrically affected pronunciation of the word
"literally" created a new catch phrase and led to hours of mirth at her
expense. The meetings with Jolene always meant a crippling headache and
a desperate need for a cocktail. D' and I were still writing what we thought
were stellar songs. After terrible meetings I could blow off steam with
Benji and a cast of rotating lovers, so everything was cool.

In September I had a brief phone conversation with a heterosexual
guy, he'd never been with another man before. Never even tried it. The
guy was in a private room at a Country Club. He decided he wanted
to experiment with another guy; he wanted to experiment with me. I
arrived at the Country Club and was met by a handsome lad in his mid-
twenties, he had dark hair, dark eyes and was quite well built. The guy
was surprisingly attractive. I think his name was Tommy or something.
Billy. Eddie. Bobby. Something like that. I followed Tommy-Billy into his
room and sat down beside a glass coffee table. Tommy-Billy was watching
straight porn on a huge television. The room was dimly lit. Tommy-Billy
had laid out a pile of cocaine on the table surface. A rolled up 20 dollar bill
rested next the powder. I looked at the drugs and smiled.

Tommy-Billy said, "I've gotta be a little fucked up to do this." He
was nervous and averted eye contact, he was blushing visibly.

Tommy-Billy knelt toward the coffee table and snorted lines of powder, one after the other. Tommy-Billy handed me the rolled up bill; he was offering me an immediate, one night escape from whatever lives we came from in the form of a pristinely white, powdered angel. I was familiar with the dance. Tommy-Billy finally looked into my eyes, his intent was so sincere; he wanted to share a secret experiment with me but he needed to self-medicate his inhibitions away. I didn't need drugs to fuck, but I accepted the bill anyway.

I inhaled a line of powder, cut to razor sharp precision. My mind was suddenly moving at 1,000 miles an hour, my heart was pounding like the fist of God was pumping to the beat of music at a dance I wasn't invited to. I foresaw how the evening would play out; I could see countless scenarios between Tommy-Billy and I. I saw the amateur video of our secret, experimental tryst playing out in grainy black and white. I looked at Tommy-Billy; he nervously covered his crotch with his hands. I had to do another line; I couldn't fly on one wing.

I stood up and told Tommy-Billy to undress, he complied; he was wearing black boxer briefs and he had shaved all of his body hair below his navel. His body was tight and toned. After we had an orgasm, Tommy-Billy asked me to stay longer. I inhaled more drugs. We fucked again. I did more drugs. We fucked again. I did more drugs. Tommy-Billy would make requests of me to do certain things while we were fornicating. I tried to comply, he was straight and this was his first time with a guy, I wanted him to enjoy it. Tommy-Billy kept asking me to be rough; the rougher I got, the more powerful his orgasm.

Tommy-Billy and I came 6 or 7 times, punctuating our depraved, sexual show-and-tell experiment with a lot of cocaine. I couldn't stop; my cock wouldn't go soft. Tommy-Billy wanted it. Tommy-Billy was astonished, he kept telling me how amazing he felt. I was kneeling beside the coffee table, my heart was pounding and my left arm was numb. I looked over at Tommy-Billy, he stroked his cock toward me; we were going to fuck again. I snorted another line and my mind sped up like a racecar, the tires in my mind spun out, burning their tread at the starting line. Tommy-Billy and I ejaculated once more.

I was wiped out and very, very high. Too high. I knew it was time to leave. I looked down at the coffee table; there was a small amount of powder left lying untouched. I asked Tommy-Billy is he was cool with me taking one more bump; he nodded. My chest begged me not to take another hit; I could feel my heart beating so hard it hurt. I had a quick flash of thought; if I overdosed at a Country Club with a supposed straight guy, he'd never call for help. Tommy-Billy would be asked who I was and what I was doing in his room. He couldn't explain the situation to police and paramedics. He'd never be able to admit that we had sex, lots of sex. If I overdosed Tommy-Billy would throw my body in a dumpster behind the main clubhouse.

Tommy-Billy disappeared around the corner, I heard water running; he was washing up, trying to rinse away his rising guilt with tap water and bar soap.

My mind was reeling, speeding too fast and begging me to stop. My chest was pounding; my left arm was numb and immobile. I knew I was on the verge of overdosing. I took one last long, deep breath, bringing the little white angel into my sinuses before standing up and smoothing out my clothes. I walked to the door and Tommy-Billy emerged and escorted me outside.

Tommy-Billy looked at me, there was a mixture of guilt and longing in his eyes as he said, "We'll never do this again."

I was cool with a one-night stand; I'd gotten everything I wanted.

I received a call from D', he was out at a club and the older girl from his previous band was there. There was an immature, cliquish mentality in the club scene, lots of slander and gossip. I was as guilty of social cannibalism as anyone else. D' was feeling vulnerable and asked Benji and I to come rally at his side. I called Benji and we headed to meet D'; we couldn't leave him all alone and unprotected at the mercy of a mean old girl. I had just enjoyed a crazy, drug fueled sexual escapade with a remorseful heterosexual at his Country Club. Now I was sitting at a nightclub, having a cocktail with two of my best mates. The alcohol helped balance out the dangerous amount of cocaine coursing through my body. I evened myself out with the help of a little vodka.

D' and I used every available second to write and record. I scribbled lyrics on gum wrappers while I drove, cocktail napkins at bars and on the backs of receipts. I'd call my cell phone and leave melodies on my voicemail, before I could forget them. Creatively, we were on fire. Jolene announced that she was pregnant; I mourned D's freedom and knew a baby would sign his death warrant as any kind of productive, ambitious artist. I kept writing and recording anyway. I still had 9 months to finish the Divine Reich album, more if Jolene suffered complications with her pregnancy. We worked late into the night, writing and recording. If we finished working early enough I'd meet Benji and we'd go out to establishments that served alcoholic beverages to homosexuals after dark.

I was working on another indie comic; I had to draw, I was happiest when I was burning the candle at both ends. I was working my day job, writing and recording an album and writing and drawing another comic. I was also partying like a rock star at every available opportunity. I slept very little but I was having an incredible time. I decided the new book would be called *Kristian 13 Presents*; it would be another anthology of short stories.

Benji was practicing with us and learning all the songs, he was working hard to be a member of the Divine Reich family. D' began socializing with Benji and I more frequently, sometimes even bringing Jolene. D' understood the importance of team building, we were collectively baptized in the fires of hedonistic nightlife. We were a tight unit, we may have been suspicious of each other and overly competitive, but when it came to the band, we were brothers. Nobody could say a word against us; we were a vicious little army, sticking up for our fellow Reich Brothers. When the assembled Reich would go out as a family, the night was pregnant with opportunities for chaos. D' was a heavy, heavy drinker, I was abusing dangerously professional amounts of drugs. Benji had a penchant for dating *much* younger guys. We were living the esteemed, enviable, treacherously thrilling rock & roll cliché. I came up with a handful of sardonic slogans, one my favorites was "Do the Reich thing."

We were toasting ourselves with a shot of Jack Daniels one night; I said, "Here's to crime!" It was a reference to Alan Moore's the Killing Joke. Goddamn comic books, I could never shake them. We adopted the phrase and used it countless times, for countless shots. It wouldn't be the first time the Joker was involved with Divine Reich.

Christopher Nolan was filming the Dark Knight with Heath Ledger and Christian Bale. I've been obsessed with Batman since before

I could read. The day the first photos were released of Heath Ledger in his Joker makeup, I was immediately fascinated. Joker has always been an intoxicating, infectious character for me. I emailed D' a link to the photos and told him we had to cover a song from Prince's 1989 Batman album; the soundtrack he'd written for Tim Burton's film. D' and I both loved the album and it had served as my introduction to Prince. My whole world revolved around Batman during the summer of 1989. The Batman album remains one of my favorite records, a naively halcyon childhood obsession.

D' and I had trouble deciding between the first two songs on the album; The Future, with its dark and egotistical nihilism, and Electric Chair, a wonderfully sleazy come on. We chose Electric Chair. By the end of the night D' had drafted the instrumentation for our version. The next evening, I recorded vocals while Benji sat outside of the vocal booth, playing the bass line over and over again.

Benji was fitting in well, even if D' was perpetually rolling his eyes at Benjamin's recycled opinions. Sometimes I joined in Ben's hazing. D' and I made up a fictional band, we gave rave reviews of the imaginary band's work. D' and I were sure Benji would run out and try to acquire every piece of music in the fictional band's catalogue, just because we said they were cool. We were testing Benji; we were fucking with him. We were dicks.

The time came to literally initiate Benjamin; he couldn't be considered one of the family till he was hazed into the Reich. D' and I agreed on Benji's initiation, we set the plan in motion on a Monday night. D' and Jolene met me as I was leaving work at the college, D' was standing at my desk, he gave me a familiar wink.

The sly little lad said, "Wanna take the edge off?"

D' materialized a pint of Jack Daniels from his coat pocket, he waved the bottle at me. D's eyes went wide as the bottle slipped from his fingers and fell on the concrete floor with a loud clatter. The college's accountant was walking by and looked back to see what had happened, D' scrambled to hide the bottle. Whiskey had spilt on the floor in front of my desk; the smell of alcohol poisoned the air. D' and I laughed, it was rare that D' would ever let any amount of alcohol escape his clutches. I left work; we took a few drinks and went to pick up Benji.

The assembled Reich drove downtown to Charlie's; the bar hosted gay Karaoke on Monday night, complete with an audience of hooting queer cowboys and their Tennessee Williams-esque fag-hags. D' and I made Benji perform Lionel Richie's "Hello". When Benjamin's turn on stage came, he performed like a seasoned torch singer, he was sheer camp. D', Jolene and I shouted and catcalled from the audience. Benji received roaring applause and the phone number of a toothless, confused cowpoke. Nothing but the best for my boys. We had cocktails; we partied. D', Benji and I returned to the stage to perform Prince's 1999 in a drunken haze. It was a good night; we were all becoming the closest of friends and partners. We were becoming a real family, a family of choice, not fate or coincidence.

We decided to dress as our cultural stereotypes for Halloween. I was a tall Teutonic and French hybrid. I was the Reich's lone white boy, my German heritage won out and I dressed as a Nazi soldier. However, my armband had a bold K in place of a swastika; the only political allegiance I'd ever acknowledge was to myself. Benji dressed as a Luchador, D' dressed as a samurai (even though he was Korean, not Japanese), and Jolene was initially going to be a fierce Blacksploitation inspired femme fatale. I loved Cleopatra Jones and Foxy Brown; I was actually quite excited that Jolene and I would share a common pop culture interest. Jolene instead dressed in an unflattering Geisha costume.

We convened at the Compound before heading to a private party at a friend's house. Some of Benji and mine's mutual friends from the gay club scene were throwing a costume party with all the trappings of the season: Jell-O shots in syringes, costume contests, Halloween themed food and drink, and a huge house to play in. D' and Jolene would attend the party with us before heading out on their own to a goth club. I wasn't down for that. I wanted to visit a few gay clubs and return to the house party after last call, I was sure to find a date for the night in the dark, spookily decorated house.

The Reich family had a drink at the Compound and then drove to the party; it was packed with costumed guests. Friends from college were there in ridiculous outfits. A few random straight girls at the party asked to take my picture with them individually. I complied. The Reich family suddenly needed to use the bathroom; we all went in unison, there was safety in numbers. The party was so packed we couldn't have gone alone if we wanted to; and wisely, no one thought I should be left unsupervised. Left to my own devices I was certain to score drugs or fornicate in the bathroom. Benji and I peed in the sink, Jolene in the toilet and D' in the shower. D' and Jolene went off on their own and Benji and I went downtown to run from club to club. We returned to the house party after last call as planned. I ended up receiving fellatio from a policeman in the basement of the house.

Weeks passed as D' and I continued to write and record, laying out a timeline in which to complete the album. Every sound was new and exciting. D' would show me the rough mix of a song he was writing and I'd return the next evening, before it was finished, with a melody and lyrical concept. Or conversely, I'd present D' with a song title and theme and he'd hurriedly compose music while I wrote lyrics. We were collaborating hard and fast, trying to best the idea we had conceived the night before. We were excited and couldn't wait to reconvene each evening to show each other what we had created.

Benji and I were at the Compound on a Sunday night, enjoying a drink that tasted like Gasoline. I was scribbling song lyrics on a paper napkin; my back had hurt all day. As the night progressed, the pain in my back grew worse. My chest felt painfully constricted and I was having difficulty breathing. Eventually I couldn't sit up straight or turn to either side. I was only comfortable doubled over. My breathing was limited to short, quick gasps; anything else was agony.

By the next morning, my condition worsened to the point of immobility. I could barely move and literally could not breath. Once again, as ever, I went to see Doctor Gale. I waited for him in the examination room; I had to rest my elbows on my knees, extending my chest and back from the fetal position caused excruciating pain. I forced air into my lungs in tiny, sharp breaths. Doctor Gale examined me, assessing the misery I was in. I had a high fever and needed to cough, which I refused to allow my body to do; the resulting spasm wracked my body with crippling pain. Doctor Gale order my chest to be X-Rayed, I was scared. Surely pain and discomfort of this caliber was an indication of something serious.

I was diagnosed with Pleurisy, an infection and swelling of the membranes surrounding your lungs, and a severe viral infection. The infection was among the most painful things I'd faced, far more painful than my tattoos and on par with, but slightly surpassing the previous year's shingles. Not enough rest, no food, too much partying and too much work had compromised my immune system, contributing to my exhaustion and susceptibility. I had been in Hell, but recovered in only a week. Doctor Gale had once again repaired me when I had broken down. Doctor Gale always fixed me when I broke.

D' flew to New York on business in early December. I was left to run the city. I exchanged emails with the manager at Tracks, the club Jarod worked for and had me banned from for life; evidently "life" was about 11 months, because that's how long my excommunication lasted. The manager asked me to come back, he said the drama with Jarod was over and should be forgiven. I made my triumphant return to Tracks on a busy Thursday, the club's all-ages night, with Benji in tow. The place was packed with chicken, young gay boys all looking for their future ex-boyfriends.

Jarod never forgave me; he was horrified that I'd been let back into the club against his wishes. His frustration was meaningless to me, Jarod never understood the importance of a story's conclusion; fairy tales are classic and legendary because they *end*. The witch dies, the star kisses the prince and it's over. The story ends.

The Reich went out together for New Years Eve, this time D' chose the main venue. We'd usher in the New Year at Vinyl, a goth club where D's friends hung out. We enjoyed a pre-game cocktail at the Compound. For me, Vinyl was a crashing bore, Benji and I were agonizingly bored as D' and Jolene minced from group to group, acting charming and serving face. I regretted going out as a group, all the drugs in the world couldn't have made Vinyl fun on New Year's Eve. As the night drew to a close, we left as a family. We were walking outside when gunshots echoed through the club's foyer. Someone was firing a gun just outside the entrance. We were finally able to leave as police set up barriers and taped off the scene of the shooting. Evidently a player for the Denver Bronco's had been partying upstairs at Vinyl, in the hip hop room, he had just been shot and killed. I remember our collective response to the death was, "We better be able to get our car out of here." We carelessly reduced the tragedy and resulting police presence to an inconvenience.

NEW YEAR'S EVE WITH DIVINE REICH
BENJI, D' AND 13
Photo by Camille

The Reich family ended up closing the night down at the Compound, D' was so drunk he could barely function. The Compound's men's room didn't have urinals; it had long, communal troughs, ideal for cruising your neighbor. D' and I had to use the bathroom, we went together. New Year's Eve ended with D' vomiting uncontrollably into a trough in the bathroom at the Compound. Several men, who I'm certain were cruising the bathroom for a last minute hook up, looked on in horror as vomit splashed everywhere. I can still picture the looks on the faces of all the shirtless, sweaty gays standing around us, those poor boys were traumatized as D' puked up his weight in alcohol and wishes for a prosperous new year! It was D's finest moment and I'd never been prouder.

I knew Divine Reich would need a live drummer to be taken seriously. Every decent band, no matter how steeped in electronics, needs a live drummer. Live percussionists fill the stage with raw energy and kinetic rhythm. Live shows are so much more visceral and engaging with live drums. I invited a design student from the college to try out for the band. His name was Jorge; he went by the nickname Whorehey, an appropriate tag for one associated with Divine Reich. Whorehey was thin and almost pretty; he dressed like an angsty teenager. I was to remain the only white boy in the Reich, the token Teutonic Caucasian in a band with an Asian and two Mexicans. Whorehey was heterosexual and a total womanizer; he carried himself like a successful rock star before he ever played a note for us. Whorehey's role would be commensurate with Benji's; they were both hired guns, meant to fill out our ranks and bolster our live presence. D' and I had each of the boys sign contracts explaining their limited involvement.

Whorehey was a hard worker who reveled in his role; he was ambitious and hungry to play with us. I was impressed by his drive and initiative, Whorehey learned the Reich material in a matter of days.

WHOREHEY, 13, D' AND BENJI
Photo by John Rose

D' and I were working on final touches to An American Tragedy, mixing and finessing the completed tracks. We began work on the publicity side of the project, hiring talented young photographers to shoot us for the accompanying album artwork. We had several photo shoots for the album. One shoot took place out on the town; I decided it would be a swell idea for a photographer to follow the Reich family around for a typical night of debauchery. The photographer watched our every move, shooting strategically whenever one of us struck a memorable pose, which was often. The Reich boys were all image conscious, vain bitches.

The Reich family and our entourage of photographers ended up at Tracks. Jarod was serving drinks behind one of the clubs many bars. One of the photographers wanted a drink; I followed him to the bar, continuing the conversation we were engaged in. The photographer was interrupted mid sentence by Jarod's barback, who had appeared beside us. The twinkish barback motioned toward me and lisped to the photographer, "I'm sorry but Jarod won't serve you because you're with *him*."

The photographer and I laughed and laughed. We patronized a female bartender with enormous breasts instead of the evidently very sensitive and grudge holding Jarod. The girl's line moved faster anyway.

In what seemed like a never-ending cavalcade of ailments, I had a persistent pain in my jaw that wouldn't go away. I went to see Doctor Gale and he advised me to see an oral surgeon. I did, and I was informed that my Wisdom Teeth were impacted, to the point where the top pair had roots penetrating my sinuses and one of the bottom pair had gotten infected, the infection was damaging my jaw bone. It was necessary to remove all four, but the top two teeth would leave gaping holes that would have to be repaired. The oral surgeon assured me I'd come through ok, he did however, have to rebuild my sinuses from the inside. The surgeon would remove the teeth, repair the sinuses and stitch soft tissue over the new sinus cavity, allowing the whole thing to grow back together nicely. Or so I hoped. I was afraid the surgery would alter the sound of my voice.

I scheduled the surgery for the Monday morning after Easter. Easter was my favorite holiday; it symbolized and celebrated resurrection. Rebirth. I came through the surgery and healed as expected. It took a few weeks to recuperate, but I was finally able to continue work on An American Tragedy.

We released our first single for the song Arcadia. I had written Arcadia to be a rallying cry for well-intended partying and like-minded hedonism. Whorehey did the design work for Arcadia's sleeve and packaging, he did a wonderful job interpreting the Reich aesthetic with a meshing of flowers, vintage porn and cold, clean lines.

The Reich boys and I planned a night out for my birthday at the end of June. The family, minus pregnant Jolene, went club hopping; we owned everything that evening. We were on the guest list everywhere and the world was ours. Divine Reich was offering Rock Star Realness to the world and everyone who was anyone on the scene knew we were about to erupt. Good or ill, they'd all soon see what Divine Reich was all about.

A DJ acquaintance of mine, Rockstar Aaron, was spinning at a club called Rockbar. As a birthday gift Aaron had purchased a copy of Mötley Crüe's *Girls, Girls, Girls* album. I knew I'd be intoxicated, celebrating the anniversary of my birth and I just *had* to hear "Dancing On Glass". We arrived at Rockbar, one of our many, many stops that night and Aaron played the song for us. While D', Benji and I danced to Mötley Crüe, Aaron bought us all Red Stripe beer. We left before we could collect the drinks. Aaron was angry at us and posted a photo of the un-ingested drinks on our fan page. As silly as it sounds, Aaron never forgave us for leaving; I don't drink beer anyway.

D' and Benji argued over who's car I would ride in to the next club.

That Sunday was Pridefest. Benji and I repeated my birthday stomp through the city. The night ended after I received fellatio in an alley behind Vinyl, the same club we had wasted New Years in. Vinyl was so much better on Sunday night, the greatest four-story gay friendly party in Denver. As a band, we played together and then we *played* together. Jorge had a lady friend named Becky who became our Girl Friday. Becky was a muse, a foil and a great accessory for the Reich. We pushed ourselves socially as much as we pushed ourselves musically, every night was New Years Eve or Mardi Gras and the next morning was the Armageddon. If the world was going to end, Divine Reich were going to go down dancing and making love.

The now complete and assembled Reich were practicing furiously;

Benji and Whorehey did a commendable job, learning all the songs and giving themselves over to the project. We were planning a tight, perfect series of sets to suit whatever crowd we happened to step in front of at any given show. With a small signal from myself or D', the band could tailor our performance to suit any individual audience.

The boys, Becky and I went out one night with stencils of the Reich's logo; I had designed a German eagle with a pentagram in place of the familiar swastika. The eagle appeared on the cover of the album, as well as t-shirts and other marketing material. The pentagram was meant sardonically. Who cares about Satanism? Divine Reich worshipped only the future, ambition, love and sex.

We went clubbing and spray-painted the Reich logo over all available surfaces. I made special effort to stencil the logo on buildings near all of our hangouts. I was marking our territory.

THE BAND THAT PLAYS TOGETHER...
Photo by Bryan Lesniewski

By the end of July the album was completed, we all agreed to gather together for a final listening before we sent it off to the manufacturers for mass production. Sadly, as the band's manager, Jolene attended the listening session. The band gathered together at D's house and listened to the record track by track as Jolene made notes. Jolene, who had never been in a band, nor written a song and was the furthest thing from creative, was taking notes to better our music.

What occurred that night could only be described as a tortuous, migraine-inducing struggle to survive till the end of the meeting. In many a dark moment, I wished my head would've just spontaneously combusted. Benji, Whorehey and I sat with D' while Jolene struggled to question aspects of the record. D' tried to interpret and translate her silly attempts to be involved in the process. Jolene demanded a slew of revisions to the songs. Benji and I would sneak a look and smirk at each other every time Jolene used the word *literally*.

In retrospect, I think Jolene just wanted to be involved and wanted to have a say in what D' did. She wanted to be one of us falcons, the majestic things she saw flying and fucking far over her head. Jolene wanted to push her weight around as the band's manager and D's company's co-owner. The only thing Jolene succeeded in doing was alienating me and to a lesser extent Benji. I can't speak for Whorehey, I was fond of him but he and I were never as close as Benji and me. Benji shared my opinion but neither he nor Whorehey could truly understand my disdain for Jolene.

Those were *my* songs a layperson was critiquing. I didn't mind the advice; I love constructive criticism, that's how artists get better. The fact was that Jolene's presence was forced on me and I didn't think she deserved to have as much control over the Reich's material as D' allowed. I left that night with a crippling headache and an ice-cold hatred for Jolene. I agreed to make only the smallest changes to the album before it was sent off for mass production.

An American Tragedy arrived in massive quantities from the manufacturers and was available for download online from Amazon.com and iTunes. I was satisfied with the accomplishment if not very, very tired. The official release date for the album was to be September 21st.

I insisted that every member of Divine Reich, myself included, sign a membership agreement in which they would agree to complete sobriety the day of any live performance. The band members could be held accountable legally and fined for any intoxicated behavior onstage. I loved a life of hedonism, but there was no place for that in the public eye. I expected professionalism and intentional showmanship onstage.

The Reich planned a warm-up show for early September; it would be Benji and Whorehey's first time onstage with the band. D' had arranged the show through some of his contacts. We were to play at a smallish, run down dive on the east side of Denver. If the bar was packed and we played well, our reputation would grow. If the bar were empty, fewer people would be there to see us possibly embarrass ourselves.

PRE-SHOW
Photo by Camille

Divine Reich was one of several bands on the bill, but we were the only *good* act. I'm not saying that because the Reich was *my* band. The other bands on the bill that night were terribly crappy goth castoffs that never stood a chance. Divine Reich were the new heroes among the Goth-Industrial Island of Misfit Toys in their corsets and tall boots; we were new stars amid the wannabes. Our turn on the rotation of bands came and we took the stage like an invading army. The Reich offered up an onslaught of sleazy electronic rock. The four of us simply dominated the stage; we collectively poured a lifetime of egotistic grandstanding and elitist posturing onto the waiting senses of what turned out to be a respectable crowd. We were a few songs into our set and I knew the machine I had built, this Divine Reich, was running like a clockwork monster. I shared a satisfied smile with D' before tearing into another song.

I noticed the bass sounded odd, looking over at Benji I realized he had one, single string on his guitar. Benjamin was so excited and was playing so aggressively he broke all but one string. The show must go on. I laughed to myself as Benji continued to thrash around on stage, we were all showmen, and I had recruited the perfect live foils in Benji and Whorehey. I stormed to the front of the stage, spinning the microphone stand in my hand like a baton. I was violently in the moment and moving in synch with the music. I raised one knee, resting my right foot on a speaker in front of me. As the song played I stamped my foot to the beat. Suddenly both my feet were at the same level and I realized I had stomped through the speaker. The show ended and applause washed over us, Benji and Whorehey surpassed my expectations and D' and I effortlessly translated our material to a live audience, as I knew we would. Even after watching me damage her sound system, the manager of the bar approached me and thanked us; she praised our performance. Benji and I left right after the show, leaving D' and Whorehey to strip down our equipment.

Divine Reich had survived its first test as a band; we had entertained a room packed with skeptical faces, we brought them to their feet and they rewarded us with thunderous applause. Benji and I went to a bar downtown to celebrate with a drink.

Tension between D', Jolene and I came to a head just before the album was released. I was called to a special, emergency meeting with the two of them. We met at a coffee shop, neutral territory. Jolene knew I was questioning her perceived authority and involvement. I knew the record would never be released if I pushed her out, Jolene would've Yoko Ono-ed D' away from the Reich. So I feigned a truce with her, biding my time and swallowing my disdain.

Divine Reich was scheduled to open for a band native to Los Angeles called Mankind Is Obsolete. The Reich arrived at the venue while the sun was still out; for the first and only time we were hours and hours early for a gig. We hung out and talked, I received several text messages from the guy I was dating at the time; his name was Michael. Not Psycho Mike-O; this was a different one. I've collected three unrelated Michaels. I was also receiving dirty text messages and pics from other people that I was sleeping with or being pursued by. Michael had no idea. I liked him; I just liked sex a lot better.

Showtime finally arrived and Divine Reich took the stage, by that performance we had perfected our show. We performed magnificently. So much so that Mankind Is Obsolete's touring photographer asked to shoot us while we played our set. I mugged to the camera, strutting across the stage like Jagger and dropping to my knees to fellate D's guitar like Ziggy. I spit a mouthful of water at Benji while he played and then threw the empty bottle at him. Benji retaliated by shoving me with his entire, huge body. We were aggressively playing to the crowd and ruling the stage, putting on a once in a lifetime show. D' and I collapsed against each other, back to back. D' played an intense solo, while I caught my breath.

The crowd loved us; that is not lip service or hyperbole. Denver had no showmen at the time. Denver had no one willing to be a rock star, no one willing to posture and thrust and revel in the love and/or hatred of the audience. For a *very* short time Divine Reich gave the city what they needed. I was signaled by the tech working the soundboard that we had time for one more song in our set. I thought I'd be a gracious guest of the headliners and introduce them. After all, their photographer had just spent an hour taking our photos. I stepped to the front of the stage and thanked the audience for their cheers. I said, "Up next are some very good friends of ours, Humanity Is Obsolete!"

I drove Divine Reich through our last song and we marched off the stage exhausted and covered in sweat. We were all buzzing; we knew we had played a slick, perfect set. Mankind Is Obsolete was lined up, waiting to take the stage as we stepped off. The lead singer, a tiny and beautiful girl, gave me a sincere look and said, "I loved what you did up there. That was great!" I thanked her and felt a wave of accomplishment wash over me. A real-life band from Los Angeles liked my delivery; the headliner, a peer from a much larger city enjoyed our show.

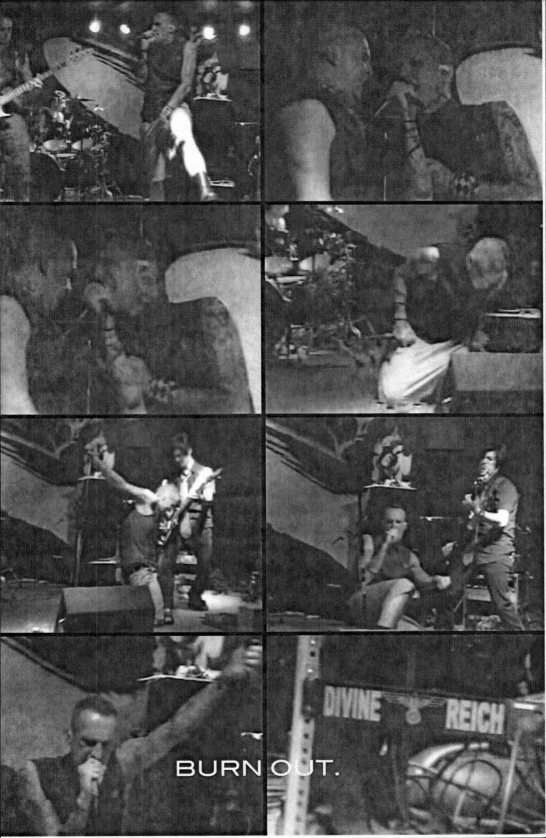

BURN OUT.

I was brought back to reality as I passed Mankind's drummer. He said, "You said our name wrong up there, but that's cool."

I felt bad for a second before walking backstage to cool down. Once again, Benji and I left immediately after our set. I was high on adrenalin and wanted to celebrate our successful show. Benji and I went club hopping and had a blast, D' called me late into the evening and told me he had forged my signature. A group of fans waited beside the stage door and had asked for our autographs. Benji and I had left of course, so D' told the fans to wait a second while he disappeared, he and Whorehey faked our collective signatures and handed them out to the thankful, blushing girls.

That was the last night we were all together and happy and civil as a band. That was the last night we were all a family. Everything ends I guess, just like fairy tales.

DO THE REICH THING
WHOREHEY, 13, D' AND BENJI
Photo by John Rose

My breaking point came on the eve of the album's release. Divine Reich was supposed to host an album release party and industry meet and greet at the Church, once again at the goddamn Church. I was at a meeting with D' and Jolene to review the press material and industry guest list for the event. I became enraged when Jolene told me she would have to approve any and all guests for the event. As always, Jolene was overstepping her boundaries and discounting even the most rudimentary sense of diplomacy. Jolene just had to be the boss of *something*. My fury grew to atomic levels when D' showed me a press release, including the band bio. My vision was obscured by violent, red rage. I saw the bio and press release through already frustrated eyes. I said nothing. I acknowledged the conversation and left.

By the next day my anger had festered into a career-breaking wrath. I had spoken to D' on several occasions from various angles, desperately trying to explain my position. When I suggested Jolene was too involved, D' would usually "accidently" let Jolene see my texts or emails, that would lead to more mistrust, and that mistrust would lead to mutual and ever mounting dislike. For some reason I fixated on the band bio from the press release.

I emailed D' telling him I was no longer willing to acknowledge or tolerate Jolene's involvement in Divine Reich or any other aspect of my work. I told D' Jolene was holding him back and alienating him from his peers and collaborators. I told D' Jolene would only ever be a suspicious and controlling wife.

I told D' Divine Reich was *my* idea, *my* band, and *my* project. *I* had found and recruited Benjamin and Whorehey; two talented musicians willing to follow *my* lead, something he was never, ever able to do without me.

I told D' he was little more than a producer who had written background tracks for me to dress up in my pomp and posturing; D' was the *background* musician who had made the *background* tracks that I forged into Divine Reich. Divine Reich was *my* words and *my* identity.

I told D' the bio on the press release was bullshit, making him sound like he was far more important than he deserved. I told D' *my* band would perform at the album release party, after that the future would be uncertain. But *I* would be the one to decide, because it was *my* band.

I said all of this to a best friend and brother. I said all of this to a collaborator I truly loved like family. I was insane with anger and aggression, I wanted to hurt D' for allowing Jolene to effect my work and I wanted to hurt Jolene simply because she was a cunt. I was drawing a line in the sand, I expected D' to fire back and respond with a vicious attack of his own. D' did the opposite; he told me he was cancelling the album release party.

D' just gave up, he didn't fight for his art, he didn't stand up to me. The album An American Tragedy would be released as planned, but it wouldn't have any press or marketing support. D' wished me luck in my future endeavors via email.

In hindsight I was an idiot. I wrote the copy for the bio on the press release myself. I was desperate for something to be mad about. I wanted something to fuel an attack against D', I wanted to punish him for the months of passive aggressive dysfunction I suffered at Jolene's hands. In truth, Jolene mattered little to me, she was insignificant in the grand scheme of things. Jolene was irrelevant; her predictable behavior simply allowed me to cast her as a villain. I had worked myself into an irrational state; Jolene was just a scapegoat.

Due to no one's fault but my own, I had pushed myself too hard for too long. I alienated my best friend. I was dangerously underweight; I was using perilous amounts of drugs. When I wasn't working on music, I was drawing. When I wasn't pursuing my creative endeavors, I was working a full time day job. I never slept. I hardly ate. I lived to work. I lived to make art and music and money. In self-inflicted exhaustion I broke down and lashed out at my closest friend, my brother. The damage was done. The damage was irreparable.

I was so exhausted and so overwhelmed that I suddenly didn't care if anyone else ever heard the songs we'd written.

I was already living the rock life, I didn't need D' or Jolene to validate that. Any kid that wants to be more than they are is a rock star. Any kid who dresses against type, any kid who does what their idiot peers consider to be stupid, silly or taboo is a rock star. Any kid who survives bullying or peer pressure is a rock star. I wanted to give the songs we had written a chance and I did. Now it was over.

The album An American Tragedy is the only surviving record of a dead civilization. It's the last recorded transmission from a spaceship just before it crashed to Earth, incinerating everyone aboard.

Chapter 25: SOMEDAY JUST BEFORE NEVER

I can't believe you haven't heard this story.

I died so often that I lost count. My deaths were many and were often due to my own self-destructive negligence, or due to my determination to have fun and get what I wanted at all costs. Thankfully Navants are quite hard to kill, most especially myself. I was blessed with perpetual resurrection.

After Divine Reich ended and the dust settled, I felt as though a weight had been lifted off my shoulders. I had graduated college with honors, I had self-published comic books, I had written and recorded an album. I modeled; I danced. I had pushed myself beyond the breaking point and was lucky enough to live to see another day.

In retrospect, my life may seem wicked, my behavior abominable, but I am *not* what I have done.

I was a monster, a vampire from space. I was a stranger in a strange world, trying to learn how to live among real people.

I had made countless mistakes and been the vilest of villains; I had been greedy. I had been silly and pretentious and a freak. I had been amorous and self indulgently sexual. I had been vain and narcissistic. But, I had paid for my villainy with life itself. My penance was served in the form of my death, experienced in nearly every possible manner. I was lucky enough to be reborn, to try to realize my potential.

I woke up from my past and felt refreshed and groggy, as if having experienced a very taxing, exhausting dream.

I was so tired of dying.

I was ready to live.

I didn't want to self medicate myself under the guise of social extremity and a night on the town. I didn't want to sell my love. I didn't want to do any of the things a villain does. I had no idea what the future would hold but I was certain of one thing, I *had* earned a future and it was clean and undiscovered. The future was a wide-open vista, a virgin country waiting to be pioneered.

I don't know how many more lives I'll have or how many more chances I'll get, but while I live I'll fight and dream and breathe and bleed.

I'll break things. I'll burn things. I'll create. I'll destroy.

I'll fall in love.

I'll try to be good.

I'll try to be brilliant.

I'll be a hero.

SOMEDAY JUST BEFORE NEVER
Photo by Johnny White and Yves Navant

Acknowledgments:

I thank Heaven for hope and Hell for burning so intensely, Dr. John Gale for keeping me alive and fixing me when I break, my holy trinity of unlikely inspirations: Prince, Morrissey and Rob Halford, the monsters of Universal and John Carpenter, against whom I've measured myself, Lilies, Mary and my beautiful and patient mum; no one else, because much of what I've done, I've done alone. History will prove me right.

Photo Credits:

Florian Bailleul: page 66
Camille: pages 67, 183, 186, 205 and 211
Victoria Coco: pages 7, 10, 57 and 61
Julian Kay: page 164
Agent Lain: pages 65, 170 and 178
Bryan Lesniewski: page 209
Yves Navant: cover and pages 63 and 64
Alexander Nevermind: pages 62, 92 and 152
Daniyil Onufrishyn: pages 70, 72 and 74
Ashley Phibes: page 143
John Rose: pages 68, 206 and 216
Kent Sanchez: page 69
Christopher Schadenfreude: pages 47, 52 and 85
Jorge Vargas and Vargas Visions: pages 214 and 215
Johnny White and Yves Navant: pages 71, 73 and 223

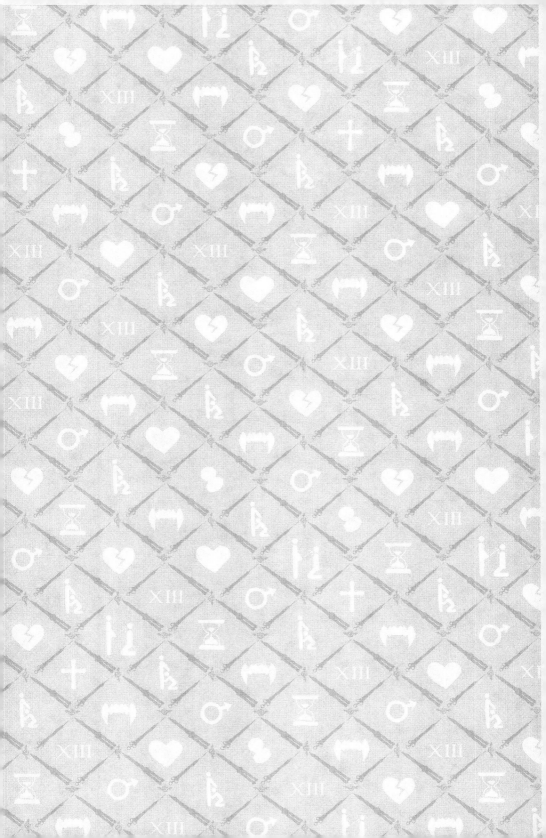

CPSIA information can be obtained at www.ICGtesting.com
Printed in the USA
LVOW060514140213

320054LV00001B/43/P